LAW AND INTERNATIONAL ORDER

LAW AND INTERNATIONAL ORDER

Proceedings of the
First European Bahá'í
Conference on Law and
International Order,
De Poort, the Netherlands
8-11 June 1995

Bahá'í
Publishing Trust

IN ASSOCIATION WITH

TÁHIRIH INSTITUUT
EDUCATIEVE INSTELLING

Law and International Order:
Proceedings of the First European Bahá'í
Conference on Law and International Order,
De Poort, the Netherlands, 8-11 June 1995

Published in association with
the Táhirih Institute

British Library Cataloguing-in-Publication Data

A catalogue record for this book
is available from the British Library

ISBN 1-870989-73-2

Designed and typeset at the Bahá'í Publishing Trust, UK

CONTENTS

Dr `Azíz Navídí (1913-87), given the title 'Shield of the Cause' by Shoghi Effendi, in recognition of his defence of the Bahá'ís in Iran.

FOREWORD

Dr `Azíz Navídí's destiny as a lawyer and defender of the Faith was shaped by a meeting with the beloved Guardian, Shoghi Effendi. While `Azíz was pioneering and serving as an Auxiliary Board Member in Europe, the Guardian advised him to study international law, which he did with distinction. After the passing of the Guardian, his loyalty transferred to the Hands of the Cause of God, who he also served diligently in different capacities. Then, with the birth of the Universal House of Justice, he continued his valiant services under their guidance, until the end of his life. Throughout these years this service was characterized by great dedication, perseverance and a complete reliance on Bahá'u'lláh. It is impossible to summarize someone's life in a few words, or to describe adequately their personal qualities, but perhaps the most significant aspect of `Azíz's character was his unswerving loyalty to the Covenant. His overriding aim was to bring happiness to the hearts of those whom he served.

The life of a lawyer may appear glamorous to some,

but `Azíz never once accepted a penny from the Cause, even though sometimes he had to stay in expensive hotels to entertain important officials. Over and over again, the Universal House of Justice would ask how much he had spent, so it could know the size of its legal budget, but he always managed politely to evade the issue. Eventually they persuaded him to send details of his expenses, which were then accepted as contributions to the Bahá'í Funds. His dedication meant, of course, many personal sacrifices. For example, he was, sadly, unable to attend his eldest daughter's wedding because of an important meeting with the President of the Central African Republic. `Azíz knew how much the Guardian loved Africa and its people, and this inspired his service on that continent. Despite the physical hardships and great frustrations his work often involved, he never complained, but rather constantly praised the steadfastness of the friends there.

Dr `Azíz Navídí was privileged to serve the Cause of Bahá'u'lláh during a critical period in the fortunes of the Bahá'í community. Recently, some of his friends reminded me of his extraordinary courage in defending the persecuted Bahá'ís of Iran. They described how he would remain calm and fearless in the courtroom, often in the knowledge that his own life was in danger. The source of this courage, I believe, was his wholehearted and constant reliance on prayer. Such reliance on spiritual guidance invites comparisons with Mullá Husayn, one of the great heroic figures of our Faith, and although this way of working may seem difficult to contemplate today, the world needs such examples.

Mrs Shamsi Navídí

THE THEME OF SERVICE IN THE EVOLVING WORLD ORDER OF BAHÁ'U'LLÁH

Kiser Barnes

The Dr 'Azíz Navídí Memorial Lecture, delivered 9 June 1995, at the First European Bahá'í Conference on Law and International Order, De Poort, the Netherlands.

IT IS AN HONOUR to participate in the First European Bahá'í Conference on Law and International Order, attended by those engaged in the study and practice of law, international relations, and Bahá'í administration, as well as by a broad spectrum of believers from the European Bahá'í community. It is a special privilege to have been asked to deliver the first Dr 'Azíz Navídí Memorial Lecture, which I have entitled 'The Theme of Service in the Evolving World Order of Bahá'u'lláh.' When I received the invitation from the Táhirih Institute, I was delighted that it had seen fit to establish this lecture in memory of a brilliant jurist, an exemplary Bahá'í, who was given the title 'Shield of the Cause' by the beloved Guardian in recognition of his courageous defence of the believers in Iran.

'Azíz Navídí was born in 1913 into a distinguished

Bahá'í family in Hamadan, Iran, and passed away in London in 1987 at the age of 74. His splendid record of service includes fifty years in the legal profession, and five distinct periods of service on three continents, in which he was in turn: a Knight of Bahá'u'lláh; attorney for the Hands of the Cause of God in the Holy Land, Custodians of the Bahá'í Faith during that 'dangerous, challenging, but obviously divinely protected period' between the death of the beloved Guardian and the election of the Universal House of Justice;[1] lawyer to the National Spiritual Assembly of Iran at a time when the Cause was under sustained and vicious attack in the land of its birth; international pioneer; Auxiliary Board member; representative of the Bahá'í International Community; legal counsel to government ministries; and incorporator of numerous National Spiritual Assemblies.

From consultations with close friends of the Dr Navídí family at the Bahá'í World Centre over what might be presented in this inaugural lecture in honour of a remarkable lawyer who was loved and admired by all who knew him, I formed the impression that, in all his work for the Cause, Dr Navídí was sustained by the realization that he was labouring for an unfolding divine system. Not only is his model of servitude to this rising order worthy of analysis at a continental conference on law and international order, but a presentation of biographical details and impressions about the late distinguished scholar of transnational law might demonstrate, to some modest degree, why a lecture has been named in his honour. Subsequent memorial lecturers may thus present entire learned expositions.

Translating vision into action

The crown of the new world system of human organization and the establishment of a global civilization is the Golden Age of the Bahá'í Faith. As Shoghi Effendi outlines in his writings, its construction is occurring in an evolutionary process, involving a number of stages, culminating in the Bahá'í world commonwealth.[2] Letters written by and on behalf of Shoghi Effendi, and the Universal House of Justice, amplify aspects of this gradual process. It includes, *inter alia*, the strengthening of the institutions of world order;[3] the unity of nations under the Lesser Peace; the establishment of a world authority, an international tribunal with binding and compulsory jurisdiction, an international executive, and a world parliament;[4] the establishment of a single code of international law;[5] and a 'Divine Economy.'[6]

This does not mean, however, that Bahá'ís are passively awaiting the inevitable efflorescence of the divine order, 'which is at once the glory and promise of this most great Dispensation'.[7] On the contrary, just as `Azíz Navídí recognized at the start of his uncommon career, participants in this historic conference realize that the theme of service fundamentally informs the system which Bahá'u'lláh has bequeathed. In our great teaching mission the entire human race is served. In educating individuals, so that nations can eventually be guided and the unity of mankind established, and in building the Bahá'í administrative order the groundwork for global civilization is being laid.

Shoghi Effendi, our 'co-sharer in the building up of the new world order which the mind of Bahá'u'lláh has visioned,'[8] fought for the future throughout his ministry.[9] Just as he generously praised and encouraged `Azíz Navídí in his richly varied and selfless toil on the continents of Asia, Europe and Africa, so he has indicated the responsibility of all believers to that Order:

> Ours, dearly-beloved co-workers, is the paramount duty to continue, with undimmed vision and unabated zeal, to assist in the final erection of that Edifice the foundations of which Bahá'u'lláh has laid in our hearts . . . [for] the realization of that Wondrous Vision which constitutes the brightest emanation of His Mind and the fairest fruit of the fairest civilization the world has yet seen.[10]

How Dr Navídí came to be a lawyer is an illuminating story. In his youth, when there were very few lawyers in Iran, he decided to enter the profession. He felt that believers should put themselves in a position where justice could be won, and where people of prominence could become acquainted with the Faith. His family background also prompted him into the field. Born into a renowned Bahá'í family in Hamadan, Persia, a centre of Jewish society and learning, his mother, Badi'ih Arjumand Navídí, was the daughter of the famous Haji Mehdi Arjumand, champion of the Faith and late Governor of the province of Hamadan. His father, Mihdi, was a well known patrician and dealt with India and the Middle East in the jewellery trade.

He earned his doctorate in law at the Sorbonne under the eminent Professor Dovenier Roussear, who supervised his doctoral thesis, 'The International Territorial Water.' In this treatise Dr Navídí appreciated that modern world conditions require the complete rethinking of public international law and the establishment of new forms of regional and global cooperation.

The international legitimization of the law, touching on international private and public legal relations, is undoubtedly a major contemporary challenge. There are those who, rooted in nineteenth century thinking, decry such an ambition as pure fantasy. But it is more fanciful to think that the present anarchy in international relations can be tolerated in the modern world. As Dr Navídí realized quite clearly, however, it is not simply a matter of replacing one national law with a uniform supranational law.

It is said that one cannot truly know oneself until one is connected to a greater purpose. Give a great work to a man of small character and vision, it is said among the Yoruba people of Nigeria, and he will reduce its abundance to his size. His enthusiasm and perseverance will be petty. His sacrifice to accomplish the task will also be trifling. Whereas, the great man, with humility and sacrifice suited to his character, will be set aflame with a vision of ultimate triumph, and will fill his life with glorious deeds.

When a child is born the parents are not satisfied with a vision that in the baby's future golden age he will be renowned for excellent achievements. They begin serving the helpless infant with love, humility, and constancy, learning as they go along, attentive to the requirements of their trust at each stage of his development. The centre of gravity in Dr Navídí's life was a commitment to building a global society. He connected his life to this ennobling purpose and set aside personal preferences. For Dr Navídí had apparently pondered the implications of world order in his heart, striven to widen his vision and deepen his comprehension of the Cause. He arose 'resolutely and unreservedly' to play his part. And he had apparently realized that: 'Time is pressing. The Divine Charger is impatient, and can tarry no longer. Ours is the duty to rush forward and, ere it is too late, win the victory.'[11] This is the theme of service which enlarges one's life, and to which I speak.

By every account, Dr Navídí was a tireless worker for divine civilization. He was conscious of his high calling and was confident in the world order-building powers which the Bahá'í Faith possesses. Labouring for the future society which is to emerge out of the chaos and confusion of the present age, His heart leaped and stirred with resolution in response to Bahá'u'lláh's summons to duty:

He Who is the Eternal Truth hath, from the Day Spring of Glory, directed His eyes towards the people of Bahá, and is addressing them in these words: 'Address yourselves to the promotion of the well-being and tranquillity of the children of men. Bend your minds and wills to the education of the peoples and kindreds of the earth, that haply the dissensions that divide it may, through the power of the Most Great Name, be blotted out from its face, and all mankind become the upholders of one Order . . .'[12]

And further,

It is incumbent upon every man of insight and understanding to strive to translate that which hath been written into reality and action . . . That one indeed is a man who, today, dedicateth himself to the service of the entire human race. The Great Being saith: Blessed and happy is he that ariseth to promote the best interests of the peoples and kindreds of the earth.[13]

Towards a programme of service

Before presenting additional perspectives which recall `Azíz Navídí as an illustrious servant of the Cause of God, I wish to note that the conference theme, 'Law and International Order,' opens the way for a deeper realization that the rising new world system has profound implications for the reorientation

7

in thinking required about law and international relations. It will be useful to keep in mind the following words of Bahá'u'lláh:

> The world's equilibrium hath been upset through the vibrating influence of this most great, this new World Order. Mankind's ordered life hath been revolutionized through the agency of this unique, this wondrous System—the like of which mortal eyes have never witnessed.'[14] And further, 'I testify that no sooner had the First Word proceeded . . . out of His mouth, and the First Call gone forth from His lips than the whole creation was revolutionized, and all that are in the heavens and all that are on earth were stirred to the depths. Through that Word the realities of all created things were shaken, were divided, separated, scattered, combined and reunited, disclosing, in both the contingent world and the heavenly kingdom, entities of a new creation . . .'[15]

Although legal systems, sciences, cultures, and even our individual thoughts and vision are limited by the stubborn operation of an old order that is in the process of being rolled up, some implications and expressions of a new arrangement that has 'shaken . . . divided, separated, [and] scattered' the realities of all created things, and 'combined and reunited' them, disclosing 'entities of a new creation,' can be explored. For example, the impact of that order, which will cause a pregnant earth to yield its 'freshest and loveliest blossoms, and the mightiest and loftiest trees to spring forth from the illumined bosom of man',[16] and bestow the most heavenly blessings on law (and, of course, on other disciplines) should be carefully explored. What are these noblest fruits, loftiest trees, enchanting blossoms, heavenly blessings which must spring from the fields of law and international relations, as a result of the new system affecting every aspect of life and social organization, including law?

Might not this conference, associated as it is with a man of action, be a catalyst for the development of specific programmes of service that would increase understanding, through Bahá'í institutions, agencies and organizations such as the Táhirih Institute, of the principles, characteristics, functions, attributes, and qualities that define the nature of the organic system? Other issues which could be addressed within the context of assisting humankind are: how can the implications of the efficacy of Bahá'í law and principles be demonstrated and applied? How can we widen our vision of the challenges facing the legal community, deepen our comprehension of Bahá'u'lláh's revelation, and assist lawyers and students in presenting the Faith to those in the legal profession? How can human resources be developed to assist Bahá'ís to analyse and explain elements that promote the rise of the divine world order, in the light of present day conditions and events, and to participate in the execution of a local and national external affairs strategy?

Further issues which could be explored include: the influence of religion in the development of international law;[17] the role of justice and equity in international law; the promotion of Bahá'í legal scholarship;[18] the support to be found in holy scripture for recognition of a universal duty, perhaps as an emerging norm of customary international law, obligation *erga omnes*, to preserve the diversity and quality of life on our planet; support for the recognition of a common law of humankind or the concept of humanity's common legal heritage, and for linking law with the idea of humankind;[19] the implications for the inevitable establishment of a single code of international law;[20] the implications of the eventual fall of racialsm and nationalism, and their supporting legal ramparts, attendant on the rise of global consciousness and planetary civilization;[21] the setting in notion of a process which would further the establishment of a permanent Bahá'í centre, academy, or institute dedicated to the study of major aspects of law and world order, including the relationship between international law and religion (possibly associated with the legacy of Dr Navídí), which could become a focus for research, conferences, seminars, undergraduate and graduate studies?

As we experience a new awakening to the implications of the near approach of the Lesser Peace, the time is favourable for urgent proclamation of the fact that, over a century ago, a plan for world order was advanced which not only anticipates many of the proposals now receiving serious consideration, but also rests upon an infallible prescription for the scourge of disunity afflicting planetary life. The moment is ripe to appreciate more deeply the world-wide sovereignty of Bahá'u'lláh, and the fundamental legal features of the international order He has proclaimed. For an essential condition in the emergence of His system in all its fullness is the recognition and acknowledgement by the peoples and nations of the character and claims of the Bahá'í Faith.[22] It will serve us well to keep in mind that the required radical transformation of society is inseparably linked with the station of Bahá'u'lláh. In this connection we would do well to recall some of His exalted names and titles, as

> none other than the One Whom posterity will acclaim, and Whom innumerable followers already recognize, as the Judge, the Lawgiver and Redeemer of all mankind, as the Organizer of the entire planet, as the Unifier of the children of men, as the Inaugurator of the long-awaited millennium, as the Originator of a new 'Universal Cycle,' as the Establisher of the Most Great Peace, as the Fountain of the Most Great Justice, as the Proclaimer of the coming of age of the entire human race, as the Creator of a new World Order, and as the Inspirer and Founder of a world civilization.
>
> . . . Who 'shall judge among the nations,'[23] . . . 'the Sun of Righteousness', who has arisen 'with healing in His wings'.[24]

11

Obviously, this is a starting point for strengthening perceptions that the Revelation of Bahá'u'lláh applies to the world of humanity, and not merely to those who believe at this time. Another important matter in a contextual approach concerns deep and ongoing consideration of the Covenant as the vehicle for the practical fulfilment of individual and collective spiritual and social duties. These points are made in this lecture with the high example of a person who realized the sanctity of the responsibilities it was his privilege to shoulder.

Often in the early stages of promising undertakings involving lawyers, participants become mired in minute details, arguments about the merits of particular legal systems, standards, principles, techniques, and the submissions of eminent publicists. Often legal authorities, methods, and approaches from the rich diversity of legal systems are treated as holy writ or controlling standards for evaluating the merits of submissions. This practice often obscures the vision that law is a servant of justice and order, and that lawyers, as servants of humanity, owe a duty to justice. The practice also engenders defensive attitudes regarding 'long-cherished ideas and time-honoured institutions,' chills the spirit of the enterprise, and frustrates sincere efforts towards formulating realistic objectives.[25] Again, the life of Dr Navídí is instructive. He was not overwhelmed by the minutiae of the law and appreciated the limitations of secular law.

`Azíz Navídí's love for justice

An aspect of the world order of Bahá'u'lláh central to this present discussion is justice, a concept essential to a new social reality. It merits close examination which, unfortunately, cannot be undertaken here. Nevertheless, Dr Navídí's heroic deeds were inspired by a high sense of justice imbibed from the Bahá'í Writings.

One of the fundamental precepts of religion is that justice is an essential attribute of God. He has sent forth His Prophets to manifest this holy standard in their teachings and lives. It is the queen of all virtues; the virtue par excellence; the most compelling sign of God's favours and commands; and the most public and legal of the virtues. Justice is also a principle of unity and order, which regulates the whole of individual and social life. It is the servant of individuals, mankind, nations, institutions, unity, law and order, and has reached the epitome of its sacred purpose as an indispensable force for the advancement of world civilization. In short, justice and world order are inseparably linked.[26]

'Know thou, of a truth,' Bahá'u'lláh significantly affirms, 'these great oppressions that have befallen the world are preparing it for the advent of the Most Great Justice.'[27] 'The light of men is justice,' He moreover states, 'Quench it not with the contrary winds of oppression and tyranny. The purpose of justice is the appearance of unity among men.'[28] 'No radiance,' He declares, 'can compare with that of justice. The organization of the world and the tranquillity of mankind depend upon it.'²⁹

During Dr Navídí's pilgrimage in 1952, he asked the beloved Guardian the meaning of Bahá'í justice. Shoghi Effendi explained to the pilgrims that, in accordance with Bahá'í law if one believer has to be sacrificed in order to uphold justice, then the individual must be sacrificed. If an entire local Bahá'í community has to be sacrificed to uphold justice, then that community must be sacrificed. If an entire national community has to be sacrificed to uphold justice then that community must be sacrificed. If the entire world community has to be sacrificed to uphold justice then the community must be sacrificed.³⁰ Dr Navídí never forgot that justice is indispensable in the affairs of mankind.

The following story is illustrative. When he was Legal Counsellor to the Ministries of Defence and Finance in Iran, Dr Navídí had to defend a man accused of embezzling a huge amount of money. He obtained an acquittal. However, before being released from jail, the man confessed his guilt. Dr Navídí went directly to the judge, and the charge was reinstated! This was equivalent, as an account of the story goes, to marching his client back into the court, apologizing to the judge, and conducting the prosecution.³¹

Nothing gives the full flavour of Dr Navídí's passion for justice as does the recognition of his obedience to the head of the Cause. He adored Shoghi Effendi. When the Guardian passed away he transferred that love and loyalty to the Hands of the Cause of God. In Africa, he related a dream he had experienced. In the dream, he was with the Guardian before a pool of vigorously boiling water which contained all sorts of deadly chemicals. Shoghi Effendi said he should immerse himself in that cauldron. Somewhat reluctant to forfeit his life, but unwilling to disobey the Guardian, he inserted a finger. The skin was immediately burned off. The Guardian indicated, no matter, he should plunge into the water. He did, and, much to his surprise and joy, was not harmed at all.

Five periods of service on three continents

`Azíz Navídí's services to the Cause, which he undertook at his own expense, covered five periods. First, in Iran, where in the 1940s and 1950s, under the aegis of the National Spiritual Assembly of Iran, he courageously defended Bahá'ís who had been imprisoned solely for their beliefs. It should be kept in mind that the modern legal system in Iran had only been established in 1910, during a critical period when the Shah attempted to wrest powers away from a powerful and cunning clergy.[32]

Still, the government was not mindful of any need to protect the Bahá'ís or their defenders. It is unlikely that Dr Navídí was ignorant of what lawyers know only too well: when the public is inflamed by prejudice and contempt and demands punishment, no matter what the offence, great or small, it thinks of only one punishment: death. Under those conditions, for a Bahá'í lawyer to defend the believers was an act of heroism, in a society where justice was utterly capricious and based upon the powers of the Shah, his appointees, the ecclesiastical and aristocratic castes. Absolute authority was in the hands of the king, the value of life was trivial and the innocent were freely seized and murdered. Yet, Dr Navídí never feared. Rather, he was the principal contact between government officials and believers.

From championing property matters to defending Bahá'ís before a primitive judiciary that prided itself on making believers food for the flames, ropes, axes, and hatred of the spiritually dead, regardless of common sentiments of justice, Dr Navídí's courage is striking. Here, once more, in the long and strange story of law, is the fearless man of God, the eloquent advocate of conviction, the towering jurist of principle, the humble legal scholar of vision representing the weak against the strong, the helpless follower of a new creed against the might of government and the self-righteousness, arrogance and hypocrisy of religious leaders.

He pleaded for the men and women of God, the flesh and blood that promote the world order of Bahá'u'lláh. He was a shield for the people of Bahá. So that, perhaps, through their love and detachment, a world might understand more fully the words of Shoghi Effendi: 'The torrents of blood [shed by the early believers in Persia] may be regarded as constituting the fertile seeds of that [Bahá'u'lláh's] World Order.'[33]

Dr Navídí stood in halls of injustice and tyranny against prosecutors who unleased the passions of the mob and stampeded the public with fear and hate. Free of charge, he represented the downtrodden and impoverished with passion and zeal. The doors to his office were always open to Muslim and Bahá'í, rich and poor. He had such high regard for God's teachings that he lived in deeds the blessed verses which balance the scales between classes. Giving a special responsibility to the rich in commands that ring with equity, Bahá'u'lláh directs:

> O ye rich ones of the earth! Flee not from the face of the poor that lieth in the dust, nay rather befriend him and suffer him to recount the tale of the woes with which God's inscrutable Decree hath caused him to be afflicted. By the righteousness of God! Whilst ye consort with him, the Concourse on high will be looking upon you, will be interceding for you, will be extolling your names and glorifying your action.[34]

Dr Navídí must have placed the needy in seats of honour in his understanding of the oneness of humankind. He was heedless of the imaginary stigma which often deters men and women of good will, and, sad to say, many lawyers, from assisting the poor, unmindful that Bahá'u'lláh Himself was called the 'Father of the Poor'[35] because of His love and care for the helpless.

However, over and above the direct assistance Dr Navídí gave his imprisoned and harassed brethren in Iran, the subject of this lecture was a 'defender of his Faith' in the manner required by the spiritual standard enunciated by `Abdu'l-Bahá:

> The second of these spiritual standards which apply to
> the possessor of knowledge is that he should be the
> defender of his faith. It is obvious that these holy words
> do not refer exclusively to searching out the implications
> of the Law, observing the forms of worship, avoiding
> greater and lesser sins, practicing the religious ordi-
> nances, and by all these methods, protecting the Faith.
> They mean rather that the whole population should be
> protected in every way; that every effort should be
> exerted to adopt a combination of all possible measures
> to raise up the Word of God, increase the number of
> believers, promote the Faith of God and exalt it and
> make it victorious . . .[36]

The second period of his service began in 1953, when he
and his wife, Shamsi, went to Monaco as pioneers. Shoghi
Effendi had earlier advised them to remain in Iran and defend
the oppressed believers in Yazd. At the completion of the
cases, and with the Guardian's approval, they pioneered to
Monaco, becoming Knights of Bahá'u'lláh. Both were very
active in the teaching work in Europe and he was appointed
to the Auxiliary Board for Protection. In this capacity he
helped many National Spiritual Assemblies with their legal
difficulties. In 1955, after a fresh outbreak of persecutions

against the Faith in Iran, which climaxed in the destruction of the Haziratu'l-Quds of Tihran, the Guardian appointed Dr Navídí a member of the commission that appealed to the United Nations.

Most lawyers do not leave their professions and their own bailiwicks to risk unknown elements in distant communities. Dr Navídí was an exception. 'Detached and unsullied' he flung away a prosperous law practice, comforts and self-interests, recalling, perhaps, Haji `Abdu'l Majid, the father of Badí', on the road to the martyrdoms at Mázindarán, flinging by the roadside his satchel of precious turquoise in response to Mullá Husayn's bidding: 'Leave behind all your belongings . . . that all may witness your renunciation of earthly things.'[37]

The third phase consisted of his work for the Hands of the Cause of God in the Holy Land, from 1957 to 1963. After Shoghi Effendi passed away, the Hands were anxious to safeguard the properties of the Cause that were registered in the name of individuals. Dr Navídí was engaged for this delicate work which required wisdom and diplomacy. He was instrumental in securing and protecting these assets and in having them registered in the name of the Faith. As the lawyer for the Hands of the Cause, he rendered the Bahá'í Faith a unique service.

In the fourth phase of his service, Dr and Mrs Navídí arose to pioneer to Mauritius in 1968. One of his first accomplishments was the registration of the National Spiritual

Assembly. This may have been the first such official registration of the Cause in Africa. From his accomplishments in Mauritius, his arena of service spread across the Indian Ocean. He went on to obtain recognition for the Faith in Reunion, Madagascar and Seychelles.

The fifth part of his service includes the period when the Universal House of Justice gave him additional responsibility to gain recognition for the Faith on the African continent. It began in 1963 and ended in 1987, when an illness he had suffered in the Congo brought about his demise. As the representative of the Bahá'í International Community in Africa, Dr Navídí was at the centre of the struggle to gain recognition for the Cause. In fashioning and perfecting the necessary legal instruments to safeguard and regulate the corporate life of Bahá'í institutions, he brought vitality and status to the Cause in many national communities, working with characteristic single-mindedness to secure the incorporation of many National Spiritual Assemblies.

The incorporation of Bahá'í institutions is a significant victory for world order. Shoghi Effendi laid great stress on the importance of Bahá'í institutions acquiring legal standing. As a lawyer, Dr Navídí realized that the incorporation of a religious association has far-reaching implications.

An incorporated body is a legal entity which is separate and distinct in law from the members who compose it or direct its affairs. The distinction know as 'legal personality' is one of the most pervading principles of law, and represents one of the greatest achievements of the legal imagination. While it had been thought only human persons could bear legal rights and duties, and other incidences of legal capacity, commonly referred to as 'legal personality,' it is now accepted that corporate personality may be conferred upon any group of persons associated for commercial or non-profit purposes. The concept is an expedient legal fiction, which was introduced, interestingly enough, in the greater part of the common law world in 1844 with the passage of the Companies Act of the United Kingdom.[38]

Nevertheless, obtaining legal personality even for commercial associations, not to mention religious bodies, is still exceedingly difficult in some developing nations. In many African countries, Dr Navídí would go to the Ministers' offices day after day, week after week, often for months, until he got what he wanted. His persistence and prayers, beseeching Bahá'u'lláh for strength and assistance, through many months of anguish, solitude, and disappointment in difficult and often inhospitable environments, won numerous recognitions for the Faith.

In one African country he had attempted to persuade an official to alter his country's harsh stance towards the Bahá'ís. He would arrive at the Minister's office when it opened and sit in the waiting room all day. He was ordered to wear a suit and tie whilst everyone else wore light tropical clothing. At the end of the day he walked back to his hotel, drenched with perspiration and completely exhausted. After three months, he felt God did not mean him to achieve his aim. He prayed ardently for guidance and decided he would leave the country. The next morning, the Minister, who had been impressed with his firm resolve, summoned him to his office and granted the Bahá'í Faith official recognition.

On another occasion he assisted the believers in an African country to achieve recognition of the Cause in a most spectacular way. The story is worth telling. Through the mischief of jealous opponents of the Cause, believers were falsely charged with opposing the government. Many were arrested. Of course, these baseless charges were soon dismissed. Nevertheless, the friends were severely restricted, watched by the police and forbidden indefinitely to meet together. In this delicate situation Dr Navídí visited the country.

As soon as he arrived, he consulted with the believers. Then, he promptly moved into the most expensive hotel, hired the very best car to be had in town, ensured that it was cleaned and polished, and rushed off in style to the Ministry of Foreign Affairs. In the Office of the Secretary-General at the Presidency, he boldly requested recognition and registration of the Faith. The file which he had prepared was reviewed by the President himself. After studying it for a few days, the President came to admire the Faith and wanted it to be established in his country. He, therefore called for a special meeting of the Council of Ministers, stated his approval of the principles of the Faith and proposed it be established. Not only was his motion passed with unanimous approval, but, at the President's instruction, the recognition was broadcasted over the radio at regular intervals.

Another significant victory that Dr Navídí won for the Cause is particularly pertinent to the theme of service and world order. This occurred in 1973 at Abidjan, Côte d'Ivoire. As the representative of the Bahá'í International Community at the United Nations's 'World Congress on World Peace through Law,' he presented the Bahá'í approach to world peace. Over two thousand leading figures from more than a hundred countries received his written statement, which was reproduced in the daily newspaper.[39]

His missions in Cameroon, Central African Republic, Chad, the Congo, Cote d'Ivoire, Gabon, Gambia, Kenya, Madagascar, Senegal, Sierra Leone, Togo, Zaire and others demonstrate Dr Navídí's absolute devotion to the Universal House of Justice, and his desire to alleviate its burden. Often he lamented to his family, from whom he was separated for up to six months: 'But the Universal House of Justice has no one else to do the job and I shall not fail it.' He constantly sought the Supreme Body's advice and, relying on its prayers and guidance, won victory upon victory.

Throughout each of these five periods runs a common theme—love for Bahá'u'lláh, love for His evolving order, faith in His assistance and confirmations, devotion to duty, persistence, and humility: the hallmarks of true servitude to the Almighty. In the path of the Beloved, Dr Navídí was a champion-builder of world order, with a share in ushering in the Millennium. His intrepid courage, his singleness of purpose, his high sense of justice and unswerving devotion marked him out as a great man with a lofty calling.

An ethic of service

I wish to summarize my impressions of some spiritual values and approaches that animated Dr Navídí's life. The recent call of the Bahá'í Faith urges the establishment of a new 'work ethic,' in which work is consciously undertaken as a form of prayer and as a means of worshipping God.[40] New insights have thus been generated for recognition, as the lives of such Bahá'í jurists as Nabíl-i-Akbar,[41] Mírzáy-i-Shírází,[42] Louis Gregory,[43] Mountfort Mills,[44] Alfred Lunt,[45] `Abdu'l-Jalíl Bey Sa`ad,[46] `Azíz Navídí, and many others, show, that the Faith's ideals of worship and service, what might be called an 'ethic of spiritual service' to humankind, has been established in the world.

Faith and vision

`Azíz Navídí realized that all the blessings which will be showered upon humanity in the fullness of Bahá'u'lláh's Manifestation, such as, the founding of a 'wondrous System' of world order with principles and laws ordained for a world civilization, the unification of mankind, the operation of the 'Most Great Justice' and a 'Divine Economy,' and the Bahá'í world commonwealth of federated nations, stem from the reality that Bahá'u'lláh is the Supreme Manifestation of God. Dr Navídí was enkindled by the knowledge that he was contributing to the creation of a divine order, by the fire of the love of God. He was deeply aware of the power of the Covenant, trusted in the assistance of Bahá'u'lláh and relied on the power of prayer and guidance from the Head of the Faith.

Commitment

He committed himself at an early age to building a new world order. He was conscious of his spiritual heritage. He expressed his commitment through the development and pursuit of realistic plans of action. He was acutely conscious of the urgency of the moment and displayed extraordinary love, courage, resourcefulness and distinction in his encounters with presidents, judges, ministers, and the common man.

Personal goals

At an early age, he learned there is nothing like goals to mobilize one's energies, focus one's efforts and evaluate one's commitment. He was a strategist who thought in terms of process and how to achieve objectives.

Deeds

His vision and understanding of the divine order were demonstrated not only in his words, but also by his deeds. He was moved by principles of justice, and by the oneness of humankind. The deeds of love and service he offered the peoples of Asia, Europe and Africa brought about legal changes for freedom of worship, and especially protection for the Bahá'ís. He effectively discharged the sacred duty that individuals and institutions have towards the poor and weak. He performed the paramount duty of building a new civilization with heroic self-sacrifice, which demonstrated tenacity of faith and the abiding value of his conviction.

Humility

He remained from his childhood until his passing, a humble, self-effacing person, acutely aware that the Blessed Beauty renders victorious whomsoever He pleases. He clearly understood that it is not just by family heritage, professional qualifications, learning, nationality, culture, or personal resources and endowments that great achievements are made. Acutely conscious of the need for divine assistance, unmatched both in reverence and determination, he would pray and meditate for hours before starting out on a mission.

Perseverance

He never took 'no' for an answer, persevering until victory was gained. Apparently he realized that, 'Difficult and delicate though be our task, the sustaining power of Bahá'u'lláh and of His Divine guidance will assuredly assist us if we follow steadfastly in His way, and strive to uphold the integrity of His laws. The light of His redeeming grace, which no earthly power can obscure, will if we persevere, illuminate our path, as we steer our course amid the snares and pitfalls of a troubled age, and will enable us to discharge our duties in a manner that would redound to the glory and the honour of His blessed Name.'[47] Dr Navídí gave generously of himself, his professional talents and spiritual strengths.

Refinement

He was a sophisticated, urbane man. Not in the corrupt sense of the term used today to express imaginary superiority over others on account of class, race, nationality, professional or educational background. It is attributed to Dr Navídí in the sense in which it is apparently used in the Most Holy Book, with implications of elegance, gracefulness, civility, diplomacy, purity of motives, and attention to duty.[48]

Conclusion

It has been a humbling experience to reflect on the life of the great jurist. But I should tell you I do not have the insight of one privileged to work with Dr Navídí. My material comes from a memorial written by his dear wife, Mrs Shamsi Navídí, to be published in a forthcoming volume of *The Bahá'í World*; the kind responses to my request for information from her and her daughter, Mrs Guilda Navídí Walker; a tribute written by her son-in-law, Dr Graham Walker;[49] and interviews with several friends of the family at the Bahá'í World Centre. I speak as an amateur observer, from a far less informed perspective than members of his family and others who laboured closely with Dr `Azíz Navídí.

He was not a distant figure. For he conveyed to all who knew him, or merely encountered him, a warmth and sympathy that was exceptional. No man whose service to the Faith included dealing with governmental officials in Africa aroused more universal admiration and affection than did Dr Navídí, for the efficacy of his consummate diplomacy in international affairs.

My view of him also derives from my own brief encounter with the man. As a law graduate awaiting admission to the practice of law and searching for the meaning of committing one's life to the service of the Cause, I sought Dr Navídí's advice on assisting him and serving the Cause. His kind response, urging me to place myself under Bahá'u'lláh's guidance, remains a precious fountain of inspiration.

I subsequently met him in Togo when he was there on a mission for the Universal House of Justice. During the noon break when governmental offices were closed, we walked up and down the beach, discussing spiritual and practical matters. Once again he emphasized the importance of enlarging my understanding of the purposes of the Faith, perseverance in action, and reliance on divine assistance.

A slender, athletic, well-dressed man, his speech was soft and eloquent. It sparkled with verses from holy scripture, withe telling analogies, and with historic examples. It carried the power of conviction; the strength heard in the lawyer's plea for justice; the pull of every appeal against grinding down the faces of the poor; the petition of humanity against forces of disunity. It was the speech of a man of wisdom, sophistication and modesty, a friend upon whom one could rely, a man of sincerity of thought, and clarity of desire, a man who was an embellishment to the fields of law and diplomacy. He seemed weary, alone and helpless. But my out-stretched hand could not be placed under the burden he bore for his Lord. Deprived of the privilege of supporting Dr Navídí in the field, I am thankful to be associated with him through this lecture.

I would not wish to end without adding a word about Mrs Shamsi Navídí. She was her husband's strongest supporter and has a share in every victory he won. Her name rests beside his on that sacred roll of honour which bears the names of the Knights of Bahá'u'lláh, deposited at the entrance to His blessed Shrine. When the history of this family is written, she will have her own special place. She accepted, with her husband, service to Bahá'u'lláh's evolving world order, described by Shoghi Effendi in the following manner: 'The exigencies of a slowly crystallizing Faith impose upon them a duty which they cannot shirk, a responsibility they cannot evade.'[50] I wish to publicly acknowledge Mrs Navídí's generous assistance in preparing this presentation.

I close with words 'Abdu'l-Bahá addressed to Shaykh Kázim-i-Samandar, which, in my judgement, apply to the subject of this memorial lecture:

O phoenix of that immortal flame kindled in the sacred Tree! Bahá'u'lláh—may my life, my soul, my spirit be offered up as a sacrifice unto His lowly servants—hath, during His last days on earth, given the most emphatic promise that, through the outpourings of the grace of God and the aid and assistance vouchsafed from His Kingdom on high, souls will arise and holy beings appear who, as stars, would adorn the firmament of divine guidance; illumine the dayspring of loving-kindness and bounty; manifest the signs of the unity of God; shine with the light of sanctity and purity; receive their full measure of divine inspiration; raise high the sacred torch of faith; stand firm as the rock and immoveable as the mountain; and grow to become luminaries in the heavens of His Revelation, mighty channels of His grace, means for the bestowal of God's bountiful care, heralds calling forth the name of the One true God, and establishers of the world's supreme foundation.

These shall labour ceaselessly, by day and by night, shall heed neither trials nor woe, shall suffer no respite in their efforts, shall seek no repose, shall disregard all ease and comfort, and, detached and unsullied, shall consecrate every fleeting moment of their lives to the diffusion of the divine fragrance and the exaltation of God's holy Word. Their faces will radiate heavenly gladness, and their hearts be filled with joy. Their souls will be inspired, and their foundation stand secure. They shall scatter in the world, and travel throughout all regions. They shall raise their voices in every assembly, and adorn and revive every gathering . . . They shall reveal the mysteries of the Kingdom, and manifest unto everyone the signs of God. They shall burn brightly even as a candle in the heart of every assembly, and beam forth as a star upon every horizon. The gentle breezes wafted from the garden of their hearts shall perfume and revive the souls of men, and the revelations of their minds, even as showers, will reinvigorate the peoples and nations of the world.

I am waiting, eagerly waiting for these holy ones to appear; and yet, how long will they delay their coming? My prayer and ardent supplication . . . is that these shining stars may soon shed their radiance upon the world, that their sacred countenances may be unveiled to mortal eyes, that the hosts of divine assistance may achieve their victory, and the billows of grace, rising from His oceans above, may flow upon all mankind. Pray ye also and supplicate unto Him that through the bountiful aid of the Ancient Beauty these souls may be unveiled to the eyes of the world.[51]

It has been my privilege to unveil to your eyes something of one who, in my estimation, was such a soul.

Notes & references

1. *The Ministry of the Custodians 1957-1963: An Account of the Stewardship of the Hands of the Cause*, with an introduction by the Hand of the Cause of God Amatu'l-Bahá Rúhíyyih K͟hánum (Haifa: Bahá'í World Centre, 1992), p. xvix. For references to Dr `Azíz Navídí, see pp. 203, 397, 423.

2. Shoghi Effendi, *The World Order of Bahá'u'lláh: Selected Letters,* 1st pocket-sized ed. (Wilmette, Ill: Bahá'í Publishing Trust, 1991), pp. 33, 24, 29, 161. See also Loni Bramson-Lerche, 'An Analysis of the Bahá'í World Order Model,' in Charles Lerche (ed.), *Emergence: Dimensions of a New World Order* (London: Bahá'í Publishing Trust, 1991), p. 1.

3. That is, the administrative order, described by Shoghi Effendi as 'not only the nucleus but the very pattern of the New World Order destined to embrace in the fullness of time the whole of mankind.' Shoghi Effendi, *World Order*, p. 144.

4. Ibid., pp. 203-4.

5. Ibid., p. 41.

6. Ibid., p. 19.

7. Ibid., p. 144.

8. Ibid., p. 161.

9. Ruhiyyih Rabbani, *The Priceless Pearl* (London: Bahá'í Publishing Trust, 1969), p. 382.

10. Shoghi Effendi, *World Order*, p. 48

11. Ibid., p. 111.

12. Bahá'u'lláh, *Gleanings from the Writings of Bahá'u'lláh*, comp. and trans. Shoghi Effendi, rev. ed. (London: Bahá'í Publishing Trust, 1978), CLVI, pp. 332-3.

13. Ibid., CXVII, p. 249.

14. Ibid., LXX, p. 135.

15. Idem, *Prayers and Meditations by Bahá'u'lláh*, comp. and trans.

Shoghi Effendi, rev. ed. (London: Bahá'í Publishing Trust, 1978), 178, p. 226.

16. Idem, *Kitáb-i-Íqán: The Book of Certitude*, trans. Shoghi Effendi, 3rd ed. (London: Bahá'í Publishing Trust, 1982), p. 31.

17. See Mark Janis (ed.), *The Influence of Religion on the Development of International Law* (Dordrecht: Martinus Nijhoff Publishers, 1991); K.N. Jayatilleke, 'The Principle of Law in Buddhist Doctrine', *Recueil Des Cours*, vol. 1 (1967), p. 445; K. Iriye, 'The Principles of International Law in Light of Confucian Doctrine', ibid., p. 1.

18. Legal scholarship has generally focused on a central core of commentary upon the products of legislative and adjudicatory activity; a body of knowledge in which academic lawyers, and some practitioners, have invoked other disciplines in their examinations of law and legal theory about the nature of legal rules and of adjudication. While Professor Lord Wedderburn had observed that this scholarship has finally broken from the 'black-letter trenches', the realization that each generation is the trustee of scholarship for the next has not dawned. Although there is merit in the position that legal scholarship must have a heavily national orientation, an international orientation has emerged. As in all disciplines, most legal scholarship is produced by young scholars excited by their explorations of new territory. It is hoped that young Bahá'í lawyers and law students will fill the vacuum that exists in Bahá'í legal scholarship. See *Scholarship: Extracts from the Writings of Bahá'u'lláh and `Abdu'l-Bahá and from the letters of Shoghi Effendi and the Universal House of Justice*, prepared by the Research Department of the Universal House of Justice (Mona Vale, NSW: Bahá'í Publications Australia, 1995), and 'Legal Scholarship in the Common Law World', *Modern Law Review*, 50 (1987).

19. See Wilfred Jenks 'The Common Law of Mankind', *Columbia Law Review*, 1958; Jones, 'Law and the Idea of Mankind', *Columbia Law Review*, 1962, p. 753.

20. Shoghi Effendi, *World Order*, p. 41. See also Martha Schweitz, 'The Kitáb-i-Aqdas: Bahá'í Law, Legitimacy, and World Order', *The Journal of Bahá'í Studies*, vol. 6, no. 1 (1994), p. 35; Brian Lepard, 'From League of Nations to World Commonwealth', in Lerche (ed.), op. cit., p. 71.

21. Shoghi Effendi, *The Promised Day is Come*, rev. ed. (Wilmette, Ill: Bahá'í Publishing Trust, 1980), p. 113.

22. Idem, *World Order*, pp. 19-20.

23. Idem, *God Passes By*, rev. ed. (Wilmette, Ill: Bahá'í Publishing Trust, 1979), pp. 93-4.

24. Ibid., p. 95.

25. 'The call of Bahá'u'lláh is primarily directed against all forms of provincialism, all insularities and prejudices. If long-cherished ideals and time-honoured institutions, if certain social assumptions and religious formula have ceased to promote the welfare of the generality of mankind, if they no longer minister to the needs of a continually evolving humanity, let them be swept away and relegated to the limbo of obsolescent and forgotten doctrines. Why should these, in a world subject to the immutable law of change and decay, be exempt from the deterioration that must needs overtake every human institution? For legal standards, political and economic theories are solely designed to safeguard the interests of humanity as a whole, and not humanity to be crucified for the preservation of the integrity of any particular law or doctrine.' (ibid. p. 42).

26. See Kiser Barnes, 'The Principle of Justice in Religion and Law: The Basis of Religious Harmony,' in J. Olupona (ed.), *Religion and Peace in Multi-Faith Nigeria* (Ife: Obafemi Awolowo University Press, 1992), p. 54.

27. Bahá'u'lláh, *Tablets of Bahá'u'lláh revealed after the Kitáb-i-Aqdas*, comp. Research Department of the Universal House of Justice, trans. Habib Taherzadeh with the assistance of a Committee at the Bahá'í

World Centre, 1st US hardcover ed. (Wilmette, Ill.: Bahá'í Publishing Trust, 1993), p. 27.

28. Shoghi Effendi, *The Advent of Divine Justice*, rev. ed. (Wilmette, Ill: Bahá'í Publishing Trust, 1984), pp. 66-7.

29. Ibid., p. 23.

30. From the pilgrim notes of Mrs Shamsi Navídí.

31. Graham Walker, 'Shield of the Cause of God,' *Bahá'í Journal*, vol. 4, no. 6 (Sep. 1987), p. 3; see also 'Loving Tribute to an Intrepid Pioneer,' *Bahá'í News*, Jan. 1988, p. 12.

32. See Guity Nashat, *The Origin of Modern Reform in Iran 1870-80* (Chicago, University Press, 1982); Bosworth and Hillenbrand (eds), *Qajar Iran: Political, Social and Cultural Change 1800-1925* (Edinburgh: Edinburgh University Press, 1983).

33. Shoghi Effendi, *God Passes By*, p. 79.

34. Bahá'u'lláh, *Gleanings*, CXLV, pp. 313-14.

35. Shoghi Effendi, *God Passes By*, p. 269.

36. `Abdu'l-Bahá, *The Secret of Divine Civilization*, trans. Marzieh Gail, 1st pocket size ed. (Wilmette, Ill: Bahá'í Publishing Trust, 1994), p. 41.

37. Nabíl-A`zam, *The Dawn-Breakers: Nabíl's Narrative of the Early Days of the Bahá'í Revelation*, translated from the original Persian by Shoghi Effendi (London: Bahá'í Publishing Trust, 1932), p. 239.

38. England's Joint Stock Companies Act 1844, 7 & 8 Vict., c. 110. There were two previous attempts in 1834 and 1837 but both were ineffectual, and the modern period of business association began with the legislation of 1844.

39. Victor de Araujo, 'The Bahá'í International Community and the United Nations 1973-1976', *The Bahá'í World: An International Record*, vol. XVI, 1973-1976 (Haifa: Bahá'í World Centre, Oxford University Press, 1978), p. 348.

40. Bahá'í International Community, *The Prosperity of Humankind*

(London: Bahá'í Publishing Trust, 1995), p. 14.

41. See H.M. Balyuzi, *Eminent Bahá'ís in the Time of Bahá'u'lláh* (Oxford: George Ronald, 1985), pp. 112-15; `Abdu'l-Bahá, *Memorials of the Faithful*, trans. and annotated Marzieh Gail (Wilmette, Ill: Bahá'í Publishing Trust, 1971), pp. 1-5.

42. Balyuzi, op. cit., pp. 251-60.

43. See Gayle Morrison, *To Move the World: Louis G. Gregory and the Advancement of Racial Unity in America* (Wilmette, Ill: Bahá'í Publishing Trust, 1982).

44. See Horace Holley, 'In Memorial: Mountfort Mills', *The Bahá'í World: A Biennial International Record*, prepared under the supervision of the National Spiritual Assembly of the Bahá'ís of the United States and Canada with the approval of Shoghi Effendi, vol. XI (103, 104, 105 and 106 of the Bahá'í Era, April 1946-1950 AD), (Wilmette, Ill: Bahá'í Publishing Committee, 1952), pp. 509-11.

45. See Louis G. Gregory and Harlan Ober, 'In Memoriam: Alfred Eastman Lunt', *The Bahá'í World: A Biennial International Record*, prepared under the supervision of the National Spiritual Assembly of the Bahá'ís of the United States and Canada with the approval of Shoghi Effendi, vol. VII (93 and 94 of the Bahá'í Era, April 1936-1938 AD), (New York: Bahá'í Publishing Committee, 1939), pp. 531-4.

46. Dhikru'llah Khadem, 'Service at the Threshold', *The Vision of Shoghi Effendi: Proceedings of the Association for Bahá'í Studies Ninth Annual Conference November 2-4, 1984, Ottawa, Canada* (Ottawa: Bahá'í Studies Publications, 1993), p. 110.

47. Shoghi Effendi, *World Order*, p. 67.

48. See Bahá'u'lláh, *The Kitáb-i-Aqdas: The Most Holy Book*, rev. ed. (London: Bahá'í Publishing Trust, 1993), pp. 74, 199, 212.

49. See Walker, op. cit.

50. Shoghi Effendi, *World Order*, p. 199.

51. `Abdu'l-Baha, *Selections from the Writings of `Abdu'l-Baha*, comp.

Research Department of the Universal House of Justice, trans. a committee at the Bahá'í World Centre and by Marzieh Gail, rev. ed. (Haifa: Bahá'í World Centre, 1982), 204, pp. 251-2.

On the passing of Dr `Azíz Navídí, the Universal House of Justice sent the following message, dated 2 July 1987:

GRIEVED PASSING DEVOTED DEDICATED SERVANT CAUSE KNIGHT BAHA'U'LLAH AZIZ NAVIDI. HIS FEARLESS DEFENCE OPPRESSED BAHA'IS CRADLE FAITH HIGHLY PRAISED BY BELOVED GUARDIAN. HIS CONTINUOUS SERVICES PIONEERING FIELD CROWNED BY OUTSTANDING SUCCESSES GAIN RECOGNITION FAITH BY MANY AFRICAN COUNTRIES OBTAINED THROUGH HIS UTTER RELIANCE BAHA'U'LLAH AND HIS INDEFATIGABLE RESOURCEFULNESS SACRIFICIAL EFFORTS. ALL SHED LUSTRE UPON HIS LOVING MEMORY. REQUESTING NATIONAL SPIRITUAL ASSEMBLY UGANDA HOLD MEMORIAL SERVICE MOTHER TEMPLE AFRICA RECOGNI-TION UNIQUE SERVICES THAT CONTINENT. ASSURE ARDENT PRAYERS PROGRESS SOUL ABHA KINGDOM. ADVISE HOLD MEMORIAL GATHERING LONDON.

CRIME AND PUNISHMENT
Bahá'í perspectives for a future criminal law

Udo Schaefer

Introduction

On the crisis of law

THE BREAKDOWN OF THE OLD ORDER and the establishment of a new one, as prophesied by Bahá'u'lláh more than a hundred years ago,[1] is an apocalyptic event which humanity is now facing. The decay of moral values, which is taking place with breathtaking speed, has encompassed everything that once seemed solid. In the final analysis, this process is due to the 'weakening of the pillars of religion',[2] to the total banishment of the metaphysical from society. Bahá'u'lláh warned of 'the corrosion of ungodliness', which 'is eating into the vitals of human society',[3] of the darkening of 'the lamps of religion', the consequence of which is 'that the lights of fairness and justice, of tranquillity and peace cease to shine':[4] 'Verily, I say, whatever hath lowered the lofty station of religion hath increased the waywardness of the wicked, and the result cannot be but anarchy.'[5]

Divine revelation was the ground on which civilization

grew. With its roots cut off from this ground, there is no hold, no support, nothing on which one can rely, nothing one can hold onto, no 'sure handle'.[6]

This decay of the value system inevitably has implications for the law, which is part of the moral order. Thus, we are facing a crisis of law, especially of criminal law, which has lost its anchor in metaphysical presumptions and premises, and is now based on mere utilitarianism. This crisis manifests itself in legal positivism, which, based solely on positive, observable, scientific facts, has cleansed law of any moral concepts: in a purely utilitarian jurisprudence; in widespread scepticism and recalcitrance towards the law;[7] in the erosion of the legal consciousness of the people, and the corruption of the sense of justice and injustice; and, last but not least, in the epidemic rise of criminality in all strata of society and the powerlessness of the judiciary in many countries.

Bahá'u'lláh has announced, and described, this crisis of law: 'Equity is rarely to be found, and justice hath ceased to exist';[8] 'the light of Justice is dimmed, and the Sun of Equity veiled from sight. The robber occupieth the seat of the protector and guard, and the position of the faithful is seized by the traitor';[9] 'Justice is, in this day, bewailing its plight, and Equity groaneth beneath the joke of oppression';[10] 'Whither are gone the equitable and the fair-minded?'[11] Whenever Bahá'u'lláh focuses on 'justice', the law is implied, since justice and law are, as Aristotle pointed out,[12] correlated.

40

Crime and punishment in legal philosophy[13]

From Antiquity, the purpose of punishment has been a subject for philosophers, theologians and jurists, and different views have been developed. There are two fundamental theories (see figures 1 and 2). According to the one, the purpose of punishment is retaliation, according to the other, prevention. Both theories are characterized by Latin formulae:

Punitur quia peccatum est

'Punishment is to be inflicted, because a crime has been committed.' Here, the view is directed to the past. Punishment is retaliation, compensation for the evil that has been committed, for violation of the law.[14] The classical definition of this principle, the *lex talionis*, is found in the Old Testament: 'life for life, eye for eye, tooth for tooth, hand for hand, foot for foot, burn for burn, wound for wound, stripe for stripe.'[15] In Roman law, too, punishment was retaliation,[16] and up to the time of the European Enlightenment this remained the prevailing purpose of punishment. According to the theocratic concept of the State, punishment could only be legitimized by divine authority. St Thomas Aquinas justified the infliction of punishment on the offender by legitimate temporal authorities.[17] The Reformers, too, justified State-inflicted punishment by reference to the divine will. The State is, according to Martin Luther, a 'minister of God',[18] ordained as the custodian of justice, whose mission is to protect the righteous against the evildoers, to deter them and put an end to their activities.[19]

> ***punitur quia peccatum est***
> *'Punishment is to be inflicted, because a crime has been committed.'*
> (Talionic principle)
> Purpose of punishment: retaliation; expiation

Fig. 1. Theory of punishment, according to the metaphysical principle of justice

This includes the right to decide over life and death. Hence (referring to Gen. 9:6), Luther justifies capital punishment: *Quicumque effuderit sanguinem humanum, illius sanguis effundetur per hominem*: 'Whoso sheddeth man's blood, by man shall his blood be shed.'[20] Authorities neglecting this mission are considered to have violated justice, and render themselves guilty in the sight of God.[21]

The philosophers who most radically advocated and formulated this idea of retaliation were Immanuel Kant and Friedrich Hegel. According to Kant, punishment 'must always be inflicted upon him [the criminal] only because he has committed a crime. . . . For if justice goes, there is no longer any value in man's living on the earth'.[22] For Kant, punishment is a requirement of justice, which is beyond all utilitarian purposes; it is a 'categorical imperative'[23] in which the essence of justice manifests itself.[24]

Goethe has poeticized the idea that punishment has a metaphysical foundation, aiming at true expiation of the evil

> ## *punitur ne peccetur*
> *'Punishment is to be inflicted that no crime will be committed'*
> Purpose of punishment: prevention by general deterrence and rehabilition of the violator

Fig. 2. Theory of punishment, according to the secular principle of utility

doer: In the famous prison scene in *Faust*, Margerethe resists Faust's attempts to save her, as her escape appears to her as a condemnable evasion of justice. She accepts her punishment, which 'saves' her: 'Nay, headman, whence hast thou this right? Whence didst thou power receive to lead me forth to death of night? . . . God's judgement, to you I have intrusted me.'[25]

Until the 1960s, Catholic[26] and Protestant[27] theology advocated retaliation and expiation as the primary purpose of punishment. Other purposes, like deterrence and the reformation of the criminal were accepted as complementary.

Nemo prudens punit quia peccatum est, sed ne peccetur[28] 'Nobody who is wise punishes because an offence has been committed, but so that none will be committed'. The other formula, which considers prevention to be the purpose of punishment, goes back to Plato and Seneca. This view is directed to the future. The purpose of punishment is prevention of crime: punishement is a prophylactic measure. This prevention is to be achieved by, on the one hand, deterrence, deriving from the penal provisions and the punishment to be expected, and, on the other hand, reformation of the delinquent, by resocialization of the law-breaker.

This idea, which can be traced back to Roman law,[29] was developed in the time of 'natural law' and the Enlightenment. The purposes of general deterrence and resocialization of the violator are not based on metaphysical presumptions, but solely on utility. The shift from the metaphysical principle of justice to utilitarian principles was in accordance with the ideas of the European Enlightenment, which aimed at the progressive secularization of the world. Representatives of this theory were such philosophers as Hugo Grotius, Samuel Pufendorf, Thomasius, Montesquieu, Voltaire and Beccaria.[30]

Today, in Western States, penal law has lost its metaphysical dimension; it has become utilitarian. Retaliation and expiation as purposes of punishment have vanished completely in modern criminal law. The German penal code of 1970, for example, makes no mention of them, and modern criminologists regard them as barbaric relics of an inhuman rigorism.[31] Among the utilitarian purposes of punishment, general deterrence is increasingly regarded with suspicion. Doubts are voiced whether the penal law and punishment have any deterring effect. It has become a secular dogma that rehabilitation and resocialization of the offender is the only legitimate goal for punishing a criminal: 'Punishment should help the delinquent to overcome his *social maladjustment*.[32] However, as the incidence of recidivism is high, there are more and more voices calling for the complete abrogation of the whole penal system. If punishment does not prevent recidivism, it is useless and should be abrogated. Progressive criminologists, who call crime 'social deviance' (thus avoiding moral disapproval), have coined the slogans 'decriminalization', 'depenalization' and 'non-stigmatization' for their programme of dismantling the penal system and replacing it with therapy and help for the criminal.[33]

Arno Plack, a philosopher who regards penal law as a 'delusional system, based on moral prejudice',[34] and who uncompromisingly calls for the complete abrogation of criminal law and of the judiciary, argues rightly when he states that:

> It will become evident that many of the changes already introduced into the doctrine of penal law and the conditions of punishment tend to have the effect of abrogating penal law itself. Those reformers who wish to render the State's penal sanctions more just and humane are not yet aware of the general tendency. The single fact that retaliation as the legitimating reason for penalty has been banned in favour of other principles demonstrates that the days of penal law are numbered. Unadulterated penal law has always been pure retaliation.[35]

Some general reflections

Let us now consider the penal implications of Bahá'u'lláh's revelation, and the prospects thereof for a future criminal law. In attempting to pursue such a project, the following must be taken into account:

1) While it is not my place to try to cram the Law of God into the Procrustean bed of historical theories of penal law, the various currents of thought in the field of legal philosophy do offer an excellent framework for the schematic presentation of the law-related contents of the revealed texts, which are not set down in any systematic order.

2) We are setting foot on virgin territory. An authorized and annotated English edition of the Kitáb-i-Aqdas has only been available since 1993, so the precise wording of the legal stipulations has been made known only recently in the West. As far as I know, no research into these stipulations has so far been conducted by scholars in the field of law. The conclusions drawn here are, therefore, certainly not to be regarded as final. This is merely an initial attempt to provide food for thought and to promote discussion in academic circles.

3) The penal provisions of the Kitáb-i-Aqdas must be seen in the context of the sort of future society envisaged by Bahá'u'lláh. Any discussion of these penalties should be prefaced with the fact that the laws in this book have been 'formulated in anticipation of a state of society'[36] which will emerge in the future, and in which the various steps in educating the populace against crime, encouraged at many

and various points in Bahá'í texts, will be operating. It is therefore envisaged that 'humanity may have reached a much higher point of evolution than at present, and the mere threat [of these punishments] may be sufficient in most cases to protect the community and protect the law from being broken.'[37] It may therefore be that the application of these penalties will be a comparatively rare event, a last resort.

4) The provisions of the Kitáb-i-Aqdas related to criminal acts are to be found in verse 19, where murder (*al-qatl*), adultery (*ziná'*),[38] backbiting and calumny are generally prohibited; verse 49, where a fine is prescribed for the adulterer; verse 45, where 'exile and imprisonment are decreed for the thief' and 'on the third offence', his stigmatization: a mark shall be placed 'upon his brow so that, thus identified, he may not be accepted in the cities of God and His countries';[39] and verse 62, where capital punishment is prescribed for those who 'intentionally destroy a house by fire' or 'deliberately take another's life'. The death penalty may be commuted to life imprisonment.

Other penalties, such as for striking and wounding a person[40] and for certain sexual acts[41] are referred to but not specified. These and other provisions of the criminal law are left to the supplementary legislation of the Universal House of Justice (and may therefore change with time, since the Universal House of Justice is empowered to repeal its own legislation). It must be emphasized that the penal stipulations of the Kitáb-i-Aqdas must be brought into force, set down in precise terms and codified by the Universal House of Justice. The characteristics of legal offences need to be exactly defined.[42] The imprecise nature of the revealed text is undoubtedly intentional. These regulations are valid for a long period, up to the next revelation, which will not take place before the passing of a thousand years.[43] The establishment of the precise terms of the criminal law by the Universal House of Justice, which can adjust these norms to the changing requirements of a particular age, guarantees that the divine law remains flexible.[44]

Perspectives of a future criminal law

The Book of God is 'guidance[45] for the God-fearing',[46] the 'Straight Path'[47] to salvation—for the individual as well as society. For the individual soul it is redemption from the bondage of 'this mortal world of dust',[48] 'from the fetters of this world',[49] from guilt and sin. However, the revelation has also a political dimension: society, the State and the law are also in need of redemption. For this reason, like the Torah and the Qur'án, Bahá'u'lláh's book of laws, the Kitáb-i-Aqdas, contains some penal provisions for a future society, basic norms indicating the rank which has been assigned in the hierarchy of values to factors such as life, marriage, property etc. These norms represent only certain fixed points, the kernel of a future criminal law, the details of which have been left open for supplementary legislation by the Universal House of Justice at a later date. Moreover, throughout the

Bahá'í scripture are to be found starting points for theological reflection on this subject, as well as occasional explicit statements regarding the deeper causes of criminality and the purpose of punishment, consideration of which is essential in order to understand the philosophical ideas underlying the penal provisions. This is all the more necessary in view of the fact that these penal laws are in sharp contrast to modern Western penal concepts and the theories of progressive criminologists.

The following sections deal with fundamental questions of penal law and punishment, and with the theological aspects of criminality.

Crime as a factor in society

In contrast to the enthusiastic expectations occasionally raised in Judaism and Christianity whereby the 'Kingdom of God on earth' will be inhabited only by angelic beings,[50] Bahá'u'lláh anticipates that even in the time of the 'Most Great Peace', the messianic era, evil will not vanish completely from the world; it will, however, lose its predominance and become something exceptional, so that the earth will no longer be the 'metropolis of Satan'.[51] There will always be people who will commit crimes; indeed, the very existence of penal law in the Kitáb-i-Aqdas, whose norms are intended for a future society, is evidence for this.

Individual moral responsibility

A presupposition of all criminal law is guilt, and guilt in turn presupposes the responsibility of the individual for his actions. People can be held to be guilty only if they had the freedom to act differently. Some schools of thought in the humanities deny the existence of free will, regarding human beings as determined by external compulsions and own basic drives, and therefore unable to act on the basis of free will. The practical consequence of such a deterministic view is the denial of personal guilt. Individuals cannot be made accountable for their actions and are thus morally exonerated; the blame for the individual's actions being shifted to structures such as the family, school or society.[52] As a result, the representatives of the deterministic schools of psychology dispute the right of the State to inflict punishment. Bahá'u'lláh, in contrast, portrays human beings as responsible creatures. Amongst all created beings 'man alone has freedom';[53] 'the power both to do good and to do evil',[54] the 'choice between justice and injustice'.[55] Thus, free will is a basic anthropological condition, a constituent element of the *conditio humana*. Therefore, one is responsible to God for one's actions, for 'every idle word',[56] indeed even for one's thoughts.[57] One's basic responsibility may be undermined by adverse mental or physical conditions, but malformations of character which result in crime are no disease; for these each individual is irrevocably responsible.

The State's responsibility

The Bahá'í teachings impart a theocratical concept of the State. Bahá'u'lláh legitimates temporal power and the penal authority of the State: 'The sovereigns on earth have been and are manifestations of the power, the grandeur and the majesty of God'.[58] Referring to statements in other scriptures,[59] Bahá'u'lláh confirms that all power is 'of God',[60] that kings and rulers should be 'the emblems of justice'[61] amongst humankind. God has committed into their hands 'the reigns of the government of the people', that they may 'rule with justice over them, safeguard the rights of the downtrodden, and punish the wrong-doers',[62] a duty for which they are responsible before God.[63]

Justitia fundamentum regnorum[64]

Justice (`adl)—according to Jewish tradition, an attribute of the Messiah,[65] according to Islamic tradition, of the Mahdí[66] —is the cardinal value of temporal power. Justice, law and order are the foundations on which Bahá'u'lláh's world order is established. The essence of justice is manifested in the 'two pillars' upon which 'the canopy of world order is upraised': 'reward and punishment'[67]—this is a fundamental principle on which order in the world depends, both at the metaphysical level and at the level of world affairs. Justice (*iustitia distributiva*) requires that punishment be inflicted for a crime committed. Conversely, the justification for the infliction of punishment is the fact that a crime has been committed. Thus, the primary purpose of punishment is retaliation for the act of injustice committed, the expiation of the perpetrator for his misdeed.[68] The talionic character[69] of the criminal law in the Kitáb-i-Aqdas is evident in the fact that the law prescribes the death penalty for murder and arson (with the alternative of life-imprisonment),[70] and that the death penalty inflicted on the arsonist shall be by burning. Punishment has thus regained an absolute rank rather than a mere relative one, oriented only towards utilitarian considerations.

In accordance with the theories of Kant and Hegel, this anchoring of criminal law in the metaphysical principle of justice does not exclude utilitarian purposes for punishment.[71] Punishment serves also 'for the security and protection of men',[72] the preservation of society which 'has the right of defence and of self-protection',[73] for some people are 'more savage . . . more vile, more cruel, more malevolent than the lower animals themselves', they 'plan to work evil, to hurt and to destroy',[74] some are 'like blood-thirsty wolves: If they see no punishment forthcoming, they will kill men merely for pleasure and diversion.'[75] Moreover, punishment has also the purpose of crime prevention by general deterrence: it causes 'the wicked to restrain their natures'.[76] Society must punish the perpetrator 'so as to warn and restrain others from committing like crimes'.[77] Even the concept of crime prevention by rehabilitation and resocialization of the offender as a purpose of punishment can be found in the Bahá'í scripture: the punishment of the thief may at first include exile,[78] thus removing the offender from his milieu, offering the chance of a new beginning, whereas stigmatization on the third offence explicitly serves to protect the public from a recidivist thief.'[79]

On the relationship between justice and love

As `Abdu'l-Bahá emphasized, 'The object of punishment is not vengeance',[80] nor is it, as is often imputed, the expression of subliminal feelings of hatred and aggression; rather it is the essence and the demand of justice. Reference to the Sermon on the Mount,[81] or, with regard to the death penalty, to the fifth commandment,[82] as reasons not to administer justice are erroneous, since the addressee of these commandments is the individual, the *homo privatus*, not the State.[83] The commandment of love (with the inherent attitudes of mercy, compassion and forgiveness) relates to the realm of interpersonal relationship, whereas the realm of order is ruled by the principle of justice.[84] The commandments of the Sermon on the Mount are not directives for political action,[85] but are a radicalized ethic for observance by the individual.[86] Just as justice without love turns into cruelty,[87] love devoid of justice is 'the mother of disintegration',[88] and becomes mere sentimentality,[89] leading eventually to the breakdown of order. The growing orientation of Western societies to the secular value of humaneness (with the inherent attitudes of forgiveness and compassion), is bound to result in the disruption of the social order. In response to those who refer in this context to God's mercy, `Abdu'l-Bahá objected that 'also justice is one of the attributes of the Lord. The tent of existence is upheld upon the pillar of justice, and not upon forgiveness.'[90] Bahá'u'lláh appears to be warning against such tendencies when He states in the Kitáb-i-Aqdas: 'Take ye hold of the precepts of God with all your strength and power, and abandon the ways of the ignorant',[91] and 'Beware lest, through compassion ye neglect to carry out the statutes of the religion of God; do that which has been bidden you by Him Who is compassionate and merciful'[92]—a warning against human arrogance in presuming to be more merciful than God, the All-Merciful.

The metaphysical dimension

Thus, Bahá'u'lláh advocates that society turns back from a criminal law with purely utilitarian motives to one which is anchored in the metaphysical. The metaphysical dimension of this law is evident, *inter alia*, in the fact that a just punishment (i.e. one inflicted in accordance with the divine law) has a metaphysical, expiatory significance for the offender, who accepts it, since its effect extends into the hereafter: 'God in his justice will impose no second penalty upon him, for divine justice would not allow that'[93]—a metaphysical principle of *ne bis in idem*, so to speak, in accordance with the Qur'ánic assurance that: 'In retaliation there is life for you'.[94]

Hence, the offender can perceive a meaning in his punishment, which is not the case when punishment is inflicted with a purely utilitarian purpose. Even a death sentence carried out in error (a strong argument put forward by opponents of capital punishment)—the worst injustice any individual on earth can suffer at the hands of those charged with the upholding of justice—loses its absolute irreparability in the face of this metaphysical dimension: God, the all-wise Lawgiver, Who is aware of the relativity of human judgements, Who therefore knows that such a risk exists, and yet, nevertheless, has commanded this punishment, will compensate the person who was falsely condemned 'a thousandfold in the next world, for this human injustice'[95]—an idea that should not be misunderstood and interpreted cynically.

Seen from this perspective, the doctrine that the only acceptable legitimation for punishment consists in the resocialization of the offender[96] is not upheld by the Bahá'í teachings. The Bahá'í position derives from a basic political concept in the Bahá'í Faith whereby the common weal and the security of the public has to be balanced against the rights of the individual.[97] Society should neither suppress the individual nor exalt him 'to the point of making him an antisocial creature, a menace to society'.[98] The doctrine of an unbridled individualism is not upheld in the Bahá'í Faith.

The fear of God

Bahá'u'lláh refers to the inevitability of penal sanctions for 'the security and protection of man',[99] without which 'the world would be disordered, and the foundations of human life would crumble'.[100] However, He regards them only as an outward instrument: they are powerless to remove the fundamental causes of criminality: 'That which guardeth and restraineth man both outwardly and inwardly hath been and is still the fear of God. It is man's true protector and his spiritual guardian'.[101] The fear of God results from the individual's spiritual responsibility before God, the conscious-ness that all one's deeds, even the secrets of the heart are 'openly manifest in the holy Presence'[102] and that each person will eventually be 'called to give account'[103] for them before God. This consciousness, together with conscience, is a control mechanism, constituting for the faithful a strong motivation to refrain from evil deeds, even when there is little likelihood of their discovery and subsequent punishment.[104]

Religion and the political world

This demonstrates the political dimension of religion, for religion is 'the chief instrument for the establishment of order in the world, and of tranquillity amongst its peoples',[105] 'a radiant light and an impregnable stronghold for the protection and welfare of the peoples in the world'.[106] Since the value system, the pivot of society, is anchored in religion, the decay of religion inevitably brings in its wake the dissolution of moral order, increasing 'waywardness of the ungodly',[107] sedition, the subversion of 'the order of things',[108] 'chaos and confusion',[109] and, eventually the end of civilization. If the fear of God is the true motivation which impels us 'to hold fast to that which is good, and to shun evil',[110] then the corollary of that is that today when 'the vitality of men's belief in God is dying out in every country',[111] criminality is spreading like an epidemic in all strata of society. Thus it is becoming increasingly evident that the global problem which threatens to devour society cannot be overcome without recourse to religious commitment and to the individual's transcendental responsibility.

Moral education

Criminal law and penal provisions are thus not, by themselves, the remedy. The solution lies in the moral healing of a society faced with loss of its defences[112] against the onslaught of crime. The establishment of moral health, which alone can ensure that crime becomes the exception, cannot, however, be achieved by State decree. Bahá'ís believe that this transformation will result, as in humankind's past upheavals, from a new faith, from the new Word of God revealed by Bahá'u'lláh, which, in the fullness of time, will bring about a 'new race of men',[113] for this Word is 'endowed with such a potency as can instill new life unto every human frame':[114] 'The Word of God, alone, can claim the distinction of being endowed with the capacity required for so great and far-reaching a change'.[115] Only the spiritual rebirth of humanity will bring about its liberation from the clutches of crime and overcome the chaotic conditions prevailing today.

The moral education of humanity, through which all are spurred on 'to acquire virtues, to gain good morals and avoid vices, so that crimes may not occur'[116] is a long-term process. A hardened criminal can only change his ways if he himself wants to change, and it is one of the tasks of religion to bring about such an individual spiritual transformation. To stand the greatest chance of success, however, the process of character training must begin in early childhood, 'for when the bough is green and tender it will grow in whatever way ye train it'.[117] Therefore 'Schools must first train the children in the principles of religion so that the Promise and the Threat recorded in the Book of God may prevent them from the things forbidden and adorn them with the mantle of the commandments'; although it is accompanied by a warning only to do this in such a measure that 'it may not injure the children by resulting in ignorant fanaticism and bigotry'.[118] Character formation is not possible without moral discipline and moral responsibility towards an omnipresent authority, something which is absent from a society which has abandoned all things metaphysical.

When 'Abdu'l-Bahá gives preference to education, enlightenment and spiritualization over 'punitive and retaliatory laws',[119] so that 'without any fear of punishment or vengeance to come, they will shun criminal acts',[120] that they will become 'enamoured with human perfections'[121] and will 'look upon the very commission of a crime as a great disgrace in itself and in itself the harshest punishment',[122] it is not perhaps the specific offender and the educative actions undertaken for that individual's rehabilitation to which he primarily refers, rather it is the long-term educative process leading to the moral reconstruction of society, which is complementary, and which should not be mistaken as an alternative to punishment. Since the penal laws of the Kitáb-i-Aqdas relate to a future condition of society, it must be borne in mind that when that future society arrives, the long process of moral education will already have been underway.

Notes & references

This paper was translated from the original German by Dr Geraldine Schuckelt.

1. 'Soon will the present-day order be rolled up, and a new one spread out in its stead.' Bahá'u'lláh, *Gleanings from the Writings of Bahá'u'lláh*, comp. and trans. Shoghi Effendi, rev. ed. (London: Bahá'í Publishing Trust, 1978), IV, p. 7; 'The Day is approaching when We will have rolled up the world and all that is therein, and spread out a new order in its stead.' (ibid., CXLIII, p. 312).

2. Idem, *Tablets of Bahá'u'lláh revealed after the Kitáb-i-Aqdas*, comp. Research Department of the Universal House of Justice, trans. Habib Taherzadeh with the assistance of a Committee at the Bahá'í World Centre, 1st US hardcover ed. (Wilmette, Ill: Bahá'í Publishing Trust, 1993), p. 64.

3. Idem, *Gleanings*, XCIX, p. 199. See also Shoghi Effendi, *The Promised Day is Come* rev. ed. (Wilmette, Ill: Bahá'í Publishing Trust, 1980), p. 117.

4. Bahá'u'lláh, *Tablets*, p. 125.

5. Idem, cited in Shoghi Effendi, *The World Order of Bahá'u'lláh: Selected Letters,* 1st pocket-sized ed. (Wilmette, Ill: Bahá'í Publishing

Trust, 1991), p. 186. Shoghi Effendi has summarized the results of the decline of religion: 'No wonder, therefore, that when . . . the light of religions is quenched in men's hearts . . . a deplorable decline in the fortunes of humanity immediately sets in, bringing in its wake all the evils which a wayward soul is capable of revealing. The perversion of human nature, the degradation of human conduct, the corruption and dis solution of human institutions reveal themselves, under such circumstances, in their worst and most revolting aspects. Human character is debased, confidence is shaken, the nerves of discipline are relaxed, the voice of human conscience is stilled, the sense of decency and shame is obscured, conceptions of duty, of solidarity, of reciprocity and loyalty are distorted, and the very feeling of peacefulness, of joy and of hope is gradually extinguished.' (ibid., p. 187).

6. The term 'sure handle' is a translation of the Arabic, `urwatu'l-wuthqá* (see Qur'án 2:57; 31:23).

7. Demonstrated by a strange attitude of many people who nowadays use the words 'law and order' only pejoratively as a political slogan to pillory political adversaries and denounce them as protagonists of ultra-conservatism, although law and order are desirable themselves, whereas the contrary, anarchy and chaos, are not in the least to be desired.

8. Bahá'u'lláh, *Epistle to the Son of the Wolf*, trans. Shoghi Effendi, 1st pocket size ed. (Wilmette, Ill: Bahá'í Publishing Trust, 1988), p. 131.

9. Idem, *Tablets*, p. 125.

10. Ibid., p. 84.

11. Ibid., p. 90. The original Arabic reads, 'aina al-`ádil wa aina al-munsif'.

12. Aristotle, *The Nicomachean Ethics*, translated with commentaries and glossary by Hippocrates G. Apostle (Dordrecht, Holland/Boston, Mas: D. Reidel, 1975), ch. V.

13. On this whole subject, see Eberhard Schmidt, *Einführung in die*

Geschichte der deutschen Strafrechtspflege, 3rd rev. ed. (Göttingen: Vandenhoeck & Ruprecht: 1965).

14. Hugo Grotius formulated '*malum passionis propter malum actionis*' ('An evil is to be inflicted because an evil has been committed'), *De iure belli*, lib. II, cap. XXII § 1,1).

15. Exod. 21:24-25.

16. '*Poena est noxae vindicta*': 'Punishment is the retaliation for a wrongful act' (Ulpian, Dig. L, XVI, 131 pr).

17. S. th. 1/II 9 qu. 46, a 6 ad 2.

18. cf. Rom. 13:4

19. Tischreden, no. 2341 and 2342, in *Dr. Martin Luthers sämmtliche Werke* (Frankfurt/M. and Erlangen), vol. 61.

20. Luther also quotes affirmatively the German proverb: 'Ein Dieb ist nirgends besser denn am Galgen, ein Mönch im Kloster, ein Fisch im Wasser' ('The best place for a thief is the gallows, as a monk belongs in a monastery and the fish in water', op. cit., no. 2342).

21. On this subject, see Luther's Lessons on Genesis in the years 1535-1545, in D. Martin *Luther's Werke*, vol. 42, p. 360; his 'Sendbrief von dem harten Büchlein wider die Bauern', in vol. 18, pp. 384-401; *Dr. Martin Luthers sämmtliche Werke* (Erlangen 1844), p. 86 ff. On the whole subject see also Eberhard Schmidt, op. cit., p. 162.

22. Immanuel Kant, *Metaphysics of Morals*, translated, with introduction and notes by Mary Gregor (New York: Cambridge University Press 1991), marginal no. 331 (p. 140 ff.).

23. Ibid.

24. The rigour of his theory is expressed in the famous statement, 'Even if civil society were to be dissolved by the consent of all its members (i.e., if a people inhabiting an island decided to separate and disperse throughout the world), the last murderer remaining in prison would first to have be executed, so that each has done to him what his deeds deserve and blood guilt does not cling to the people for not having

insisted upon this punishment; for otherwise the people can be regarded as collaborators in this public violation of justice.' (ibid., marginal no. 333 [p. 142]).

25. Geothe, *Faust*, part 1 (New York: Philosophical Library, 1958).

26. The renowned Catholic encyclopaedia, *Lexikon für Theologie und Kirche* (begründet von Dr. Michael Buchberger, Freiburg, zweite, völlig neu bearbeitete Auflage 1957, Sonderausgabe 1986), advocates retaliation as the purpose of punishment, quoting the formula: '*Punitur quia peccatum est.*'

27. Paul Althaus, 'Die Todesstrafe als Problem der christlichen Ethik', in *Sitzungsberichte der Bayerischen Akademie der Wissenschaften* (Phil.-hist. Klasse, Munich, 1955), p. 21.

28. The shorter version is '*Punitur, ne peccetur*': 'Punishment is to be inflicted that no crime will be committed'.

29. '*Exemplo deterriti delinquunt minus*' (Dig. 48, 19, 6 § 1 [Ulpian]: '*Poena ad paucos, ut metus ad omnia perveneat*' ('They who are deterred by examples commit less crimes', 'Some must be punished in order to frighten all.').

30. Concerning Cesare Beccaria (1738-94), Immanuel Kant mockingly remarked, 'in opposition to this the Marchese Beccaria, moved by overly compassionate feelings of an affected humanity (*compassibilitas*), has put forward his assertion that any capital punishment is wrongful because it could not be contained in the original civil contract. . . . This is all sophistry and juristic trickery' (Kant, op. cit., p. 143).

31. cf. Ulrich Klug, 'Abschied von Kant und Hegel', in Ulrich Klug, *Skeptische Rechtsphilosophie und humanes Strafrecht*, vol. 2 (Berlin-Heidelberg-New York: Springer, 1981), pp. 149-54.

32. Heinz Zipf, *Die Strafzumessung* (Heidelberg-Karlsruhe: Müller, Juristischer Verlag, 1977), p. 52.

33. See Working Paper prepared by the Secretary's Office for the Sixth

UNO-Congress on Crime and Crime Prevention in Milan in 1985 (A/CONF. 121/7 [17. April 1985] nos. 19, 13, 18, 21, 32, 34, 36, 69, 70).

34. Arno Plack, *Plädoyer für die Abschaffung des Strafrechts* (Mnich: List Verlag, 1974), p. 19. Translated for this paper by Dr Geraldine Schuckelt. For more details on this subject see Udo Schaefer, *The Imperishable Dominion: The Bahá'í Faith and the Future of Mankind* (Oxford: George Ronald Publisher, 1983), p. 49 ff., 183 ff.

35. Plack, op. cit., p. 7.

36. Shoghi Effendi, quoted in introduction to Bahá'u'lláh, *The Kitáb-i-Aqdas: The Most Holy Book*, rev. ed. (London: Bahá'í Publishing Trust, 1993), p. 6 ff.

37. Idem, quoted in Helen Bassett Hornby (comp.), *Lights of Guidance: A Bahá'í Reference File*, 3rd rev. ed. (New Delhi: Bahá'í Publishing Trust, 1994), no. 1198, p. 358.

38. cf. Bahá'u'lláh, Kitáb-i-Aqdas, note 77, p. 200.

39. cf. ibid., note 71, p. 198.

40. Ibid., 56. Numbers not preceded by 'p.', refer to numbered paragraphs in the published text of the Kitáb-i-Aqdas.

41. Ibid., 'Questions and Answers', 49.

42. What are the legal characteristics of theft? What constitutes the 'third offence'? For which cases of arson is the death penalty to be applied, and for which life imprisonment? Which cases fall under the term *ziná'*, and so on.

43. See Bahá'u'lláh, Kitáb-i-Aqdas, 37.

44. For more detail on this subject see U. Schaefer, N. Towfigh, U. Gollmer, *Desinformation als Methode. Die Baháismus-Monographie des F. Ficicchia* (Hildesheim: Olms-Verlag, 1995), pp. 267 ff., 557.

45. Translated from the Arabic, *Hudá*, from *hadá*: to guide, lead in the right way, direct aright (cf. Qur'án 2:5; 16:38, 97, 120, 159, 175, 185; 3:4, 73, 96 etc.; Bahá'u'lláh, *Gleanings*, XXVII, p. 67; XXIX, p. 70; L,

p. 102-3; CXV, pp. 239-40; CXXV, pp. 266-7; idem, *Tablets*, p. 169.

46. Qur'án 2:2.

47. Translated from the Arabic, *as-sirátu'l mustaqím* (Qur'án 1:6; Bahá'u'lláh, Kitáb-i-Aqdas, 14, 186).

48. Bahá'u'lláh, *The Hidden Words*, trans. Shoghi Effendi with the assistance of some English friends (London: Nightingale Books, 1992), p. 43.

49. Ibid. 14; cf. ibid. p. 63; idem, *Gleanings*, XLV, p. 99; CXXVIII, pp. 274-5; `Abdu'l-Bahá, *Paris Talks: Addresses Given by `Abdu'l-Bahá in 1911*, 12th rev. ed. (London: Bahá'í Publishing Trust, 1995), 3:7, p. 7.

50. See Isa. 11:9.

51. Bahá'u'lláh, *Tablets*, p. 177.

52. The theory of psychoanalysis holds that conscious actions are directed from depths of which the individual is unconscious. Thus, as he cannot be blamed for his actions, there can be no guilt, only failure. Behaviourism must also be mentioned in this context—see B. F. Skinner, *Beyond Freedom and Dignity* (Harmondsworth: Penguin, 1971); see also Jacques Monod, *Chance and Necessity: An Essay on the Natural Philosophy of Modern Biology* trans. from the French by Austryn Wainhouse (New York: Vintage Books, 1972).

53. `Abdu'l-Bahá, *Paris Talks*, 11:6, p. 32; 9:18, p. 28.

54. Ibid., 18:3, pp. 55-6.

55. Ibid., 49:16, p. 166.

56. Matt. 12:36.

57. Bahá'u'lláh, *The Hidden Words*, pp. 13, 65, 76; idem, *Tablets*, p. 189; Qur'án 17:4; 6:120.

58. Bahá'u'lláh, *Epistle*, p. 89.

59. See Matt. 22:21; Rom. 13:1 ff; Qur'án 4:59.

60. Bahá'u'lláh, *Epistle*, p. 91; idem, *Gleanings*, CII, pp. 205-6.

61. Ibid., CXVIII, p. 250.

62. Ibid., CXVI, p. 246; see also idem, Kitáb-i-Aqdas, 88.

63. Gleanings, CXVI, p. 246.

64. 'Justice is the foundation of temporal power'. This sentence originates from Antiquity (Cicero, Sallust, Vergil, although it cannot be determined who formulated it. It was the motto of Emperor Francis I of Austria [1804-35]).

65. Isa. 11:5; 26:10; 32:7; Ps. 85:11; Micah 4:3.

66. See C. E. Bosworth, E. van Donzel, W. P. Heinrichs and the late Ch. Pellat (ed's), *Shorter Encyclopaedia of Islam*, new ed. (Leiden-New York: E. J. Brill, 1961), p. 312.

67. Bahá'u'lláh, *Tablets*, pp. 126, 129, 27, 164.

68. Qur'án 5:38; see `Abdu'l-Bahá, *Selections from the Writings of `Abdu'l-Bahá*, comp. Research Department of the Universal House of Justice, trans. a committee at the Bahá'í World Centre and by Marzieh Gail, rev. ed. (Haifa: Bahá'í World Centre, 1982), 152, p. 179; see also idem, *Some Answered Questions*, comp. and trans. Laura Clifford Barney, 1st pocket size ed. (Wilmette, Ill: Bahá'í Publishing Trust, 1984), p. 268.

69. See Ex. 21:24-5; Lev. 24:19-21.

70. Bahá'u'lláh, Kitáb-i-Aqdas, 62; ibid., Questions and Answers, 86, 87.

71. See Heiner Bielefeldt, 'Strafrechtliche Gerechtigkeit als Anspruch an den endlichen Menschen. Zu Kants kritischer Begründung des Strafrechts', in *Goltdammer's Archiv für Strafrecht*, p. 115.

72. Bahá'u'lláh, *Tablets*, p. 93; `Abdu'l-Bahá, *Some Answered Questions*, p. 268.

73. Ibid., p. 269.

74. Idem, *Paris Talks*, 31:6, p. 97.

75. Idem, *Some Answered Questions*, p. 269; idem, *Selections*, 138, p. 158; similarly Aristotle: 'Peior enim est malus homo quam bestia et plus nocet': 'An evil man is worse than a beast and does more harm'

(op. cit., VII, 7 1150a); see also Thomas Aquinas, *Summa theologiae*, in *S. Thomae Aquinatis Opera Omnia Bd. 2: Summa contra Gentiles; Summa Theologiae, Prima Pars, Prima Pars secundae, Tertia Pars* (Stuttgart-Bad Cannstatt: Frommann-Holzboog, 1980), II-II, q 64a 2 ad 3.

76. Bahá'u'lláh, *Tablets*, p. 164.

77. `Abdu'l-Bahá, *Some Answered Questions*, p. 268.

78. Bahá'u'lláh, Kitáb-i-Aqdas, 45.

79. The principal purpose of the fine imposed in the Kitáb-i-Aqdas on every adulterer and every adulteress is, according to `Abdu'l-Bahá, their social stigmatization, 'the exposure of the offenders -- that they are shamed and disgraced in the eyes of society. He affirms that such exposure is in itself the greatest punishment' (Kitáb-i-Aqdas, note 77 [p. 200]).

80. `Abdu'l-Bahá, *Paris Talks*, 47:3, p. 160.

81. Matt. 5:44; 6:12.

82. Exod. 20:13.

83. On this subject, see Martin Luther, *Dr. Martin Luthers sämmtliche Werke*, vol. 36, p. 86 ff.

84. `Abdu'l-Bahá, *Some Answered Questions*, p. 270.

85. Ibid.

86. And, as such, are also present in the Bahá'í teachings; see ibid., pp. 269-70.

87. Thomas Aquinas, *Catena aurea in Matthaeum* (In Matth.), in *S. Thomae Aquinatis Opera Omnia, vol. 5: Commentaria in Scripturas* (Stuttgart-Bad Cannstatt: Friedrich Frommann Verlag Günther Holzbook KG, 1980), 5,2.

88. Ibid.

89. 'Love which is not just in the world of institutions is sentimentality. And sentimentality, feelings for feeling's sake, is the poison the solvent which destroys all institutions of justice.' Emil Brunner, *Justice and the*

Social Order (New York: Harper & Brothers, 1945), p. 129. This book is a thorough investigation of the relationship between love and justice. See also endnote 44 above.

90. `Abdu'l-Bahá, *Some Answered Questions*, p. 270.

91. Bahá'u'lláh, Kitáb-i-Aqdas, 62.

92. Ibid., 45; cf. Qur'án 24:2.

93. `Abdu'l-Bahá, *Selections*, 152, p. 179.

94. Qur'án 2:179.

95. Shoghi Effendi, in the Kitáb-i-Aqdas, note 86, p. 204.

96. With the practical consequence that even dangerous criminals serving life sentences should have the chance of eventual release.

97. See `Abdu'l-Bahá, *Paris Talks*, 47:5, p. 160.

98. Shoghi Effendi, *The Unfolding Destiny of the British Bahá'í Community: A Compilation of Some of the Letters and Cables of the Beloved Guardian Addressed to the British Bahá'í Community* (London: Bahá'í Publishing Trust, 1981), p. 436.

99. Bahá'u'lláh, *Tablets*, p. 93.

100. `Abdu'l-Bahá, *Some Answered Questions*, p. 270.

101. Bahá'u'lláh, *Tablets*, p. 93.

102. Idem, *The Hidden Words*, p. 76; idem, *Gleanings*, LXXVII, pp. 148-9; Qur'án 50:16.

103. Bahá'u'lláh, *The Hidden Words*, p. 13.

104. `Abdu'l-Bahá, *Selections*, 227, p. 302.

105. Bahá'u'lláh, *Epistle*, p. 28.

106. Idem, *Tablets*, p. 125.

107. Ibid., p. 63 ff..

108. `Abdu'l-Bahá, *Selections*, 227 p. 302 f.

109. Bahá'u'lláh, *Epistle*, p. 28; idem, *Tablets*, pp. 63 ff.; 125.

110. Ibid.

111. Idem, *Gleanings*, XCIX, p. 199.

112. In the original German, 'Immunität'.

113. Shoghi Effendi, *The Advent of Divine Justice*, rev. ed. (Wilmette, Ill: Bahá'í Publishing Trust, 1984), p. 16.

114. Bahá'u'lláh, *Gleanings*, LXXIV, p. 141.

115. Ibid., XCIX, p. 199.

116. `Abdu'l-Bahá, *Some Answered Questions*, p. 271.

117. Idem, *Selections*, 95, p. 125.

118. Bahá'u'lláh, *Tablets*, p. 68.

119. `Abdu'l-Bahá, *Selections*, 105, pp. 132-3; idem., *Some Answered Questions*, p. 271.

120. Idem, *Selections*, 105, pp. 132-3.

121. Ibid.

122. Ibid.

THE NATURE OF BAHÁ'Í LAW

Kiser Barnes

T HE REVELATION OF BAHÁ'U'LLÁH for the achievement of organic unity among peoples and nations presents the most promising opportunity thus far in history for obtaining a fuller understanding of the nature of divine law. While Bahá'í standards reflect the fundamental character of all divinely revealed precepts, this paper will examine some special features of that law, focusing on Bahá'í law as a symbol of God's 'greatest bounty' to humanity, and its relation to the scope and purpose of the Bahá'í Revelation. Some aspects of the law which anticipate responsibilities and duties of States in the unfolding of the new world order are also explored. Despite its tentative nature and limited scope, it is to be hoped that this present study, might provide a useful perspective of the intent and policy of Bahá'í law.

This presentation has been undertaken against the background of the Universal House of Justice's statement that the Kitáb-i-Aqdas,[1] the 'chief repository of His [Bahá'u'lláh's] laws', characterized by it as 'a Book of . . . indescribable Holiness', symbolizes 'a source of God's greatest Bounty to His creatures'; 'the incomparable greatness of the Revelation of Bahá'u'lláh'; and the heart of 'a vast process of individual and community development which must certainly exert an increasingly powerful, transformative effect on peoples and nations'.[2] These three qualities, and other descriptions of the Kitáb-i-Aqdas, are treated as applying, by inference, to the compendious term 'Bahá'í law' throughout this paper.

The 'phenomenal importance' of the Kitáb-i-Aqdas, with its implications for the entire corpus of Bahá'í law, has been described as

> an importance which staggers the mind when viewed in light of the realization that this Book is, in the words of Shoghi Effendi, the 'principle repository of that Law which the Prophet Isaiah had anticipated, and which the writer of the Apocalypse had described as the "new heaven" and the "new earth," as "the Tabernacle of God" . . . ' Such metaphors of hope have been recited from sacred scriptures down the ages, have fired the imagination and excited the expectations of unnumbered generations, and now, at long last, in this new Dispensation, have been given tangible form by the Promised One of All Ages in this Mother Book of His Revelation.[3]

'a source of God's greatest bounty to His creatures'

The word 'law' is a term of infinite inexactitude, one of the most ambivalent words in the English language. Scholars, lawyers and laymen have fretted over its meaning. However defined, law, as a social phenomenon, exists on three distinct levels of abstraction: the metaphysical level of ideals and ideas—such as God's law, natural law, principles, the law of supply and demand, the law of unity, the law of consultation, the law of service, the law of love etc. Secondly, it exists on the more tangible level of legal institutions—such as courts, juries, legislatures, formal rules (primary and secondary, pertaining to specific legal issues, such as contract law, criminal law, constitutional law, tax law etc.), which collectively make up a legal system. It exists also on the human level of persons subject to law, with ideas about law, and occupying positions within legal institutions.

While these levels are brought together in the Bahá'í Writings, this paper focuses primarily on ideas about divine law, with a presentation of some tangible rules in Bahá'í law. Before embarking upon a survey of some features of these prescripts, it is necessary to have a clear understanding of the nature of divine law, bearing in mind that Bahá'í law is fundamentally consistent with its quality. All divinely revealed law represents a compelling intervention of God, through His Mouthpiece and Lawgiver, in the affairs of humanity. It is a direct emanation from the Divine Lawgiver and beyond the law of any secular authority; a mighty civilizing and liberating force in the history of humankind; the 'remedy and treatment' against the 'violent poison' of the disease of disunity;[4] the source of fundamental change; an establisher of a power of discrimination between truth and error; a justification for legal and social actions; the means for the attainment of justice and equity, resolution of conflicts, and protection of interests; a means of social control and a coercive order of reward and punishment, suitable and adapted to the needs and requirements of a particular age;[5] and an essential part of the religion of God.[6] The primary purpose of divine law 'is to bring about happiness in the after life and civilization and refinement of character in this'.[7]

These sacred commands, prohibitions and ordinances, been progressively and successively revealed in each Dispensation, are conclusive proof that the Prophets possess the greatest authority the Almighty has conferred upon a few chosen Servants. And this commanding authority to abrogate laws by which peoples and nations have been disciplined and guided for centuries is incontrovertible evidence that: 'The highest station, the supreme sphere, the noblest, most sublime position in creation, whether visible or invisible, whether alpha or omega, is that of the Prophets of God'.[8] These standards have an unconditional, unchallengeable, binding character over the faithful,[9] and conform perfectly with the requirements and capacities of the age.[10]

Divine law fosters the spiritual development of both the individual and humankind as a whole, leads to the cultural attainment of the mind,[11] and establishes a basis for moral character and spirituality.[12] It promotes unity and order and prohibits socially condemnable behaviour. It gives new life and vitality to a spiritually dead society, and eventually reflects the soul of a society through its power to educate, guide lives and mould behaviour.[13]

In the case of Bahá'í law, a distinguishing feature is the two categories of divine law: revealed law and legislation. The latter involves specific enactments by the Universal House of Justice.[14] Another unique feature is that the Writings of Bahá'u'lláh and His successors are replete with symbolic terms and analogies depicting the nature and station of the law. These terms need to be better known, more frequently used, and much more fully examined.

Although it is unlikely, and, indeed, it appears unimportant, whether consensus will be reached on the possible meanings of the symbolism, it is, however, important to keep in mind that the Bahá'í Writings indicate that the fundamental character of the Law of Bahá'u'lláh is to: obtain the victory of the Cause of God;[15] demonstrate the unchallengeable authority of the Supreme Manifestation of God;[16] fulfil the 'divine purpose for this age, which is no less than the establishment of the reign of divine love, justice, and wisdom in the world, under and in conformity to the Divine Law';[17] establish and promote a divine civilization;[18] establish the 'essence of justice';[19] achieve the spiritual well-being and development of humanity and educate humankind in righteousness;[20] lay an enduring foundation for the 'wellspring of life unto the world';[21] vest responsibilities and duties in individuals, peoples and nations on the basis of 'the resolution of truth, reason and justice';[22] guide humankind to the straight path;[23]

quicken the hearts;[24] present the counsels and bounties of God;[25] rejoice the heart and brighten the eyes;[26] establish order and security;[27] protect the world and safeguard its people;[28] establish and train humanity in justice;[29] effect a fundamental change in the world;[30] establish a legal basis for claims and justifications for actions;[31] protect and elevate the station of man;[32] present what will profit humankind;[33] enable humankind to attain unto 'perfect liberty';[34] engender love, unity, peace, harmony and prosperity among peoples and nations;[35] and address

> the needs of the entire human family. . . . gradually [unveil] the significance of the new levels of knowledge and behaviour to which the peoples of the world are being called. . . . serve the manifold purposes of bringing tranquillity to human society, raising the standard of human behaviour, increasing the range of human understanding, and spiritualizing the life of each and all.[36]

Although authorities are learning they cannot devolve upon secular law the entire burden of social control, the role religion must play in conjunction with law in reversing the global blight of corruption and lawlessness is not yet acknowledged. Divine law is closely intertwined with religion, and both are considered the expression of God's will and justice. On this point Bahá'u'lláh has revealed:

The religion of God and His divine law are the most potent instruments and the surest of all means for the dawning of the light of unity amongst men. The progress of the world, the development of nations, the tranquillity of peoples, and the peace of all who dwell on earth are among the principles and ordinances of God. Religion bestoweth upon man the most precious of all gifts, offereth the cup of prosperity, imparteth eternal life, and showereth imperishable benefits upon mankind.[37]

Turning now to consider some of the 'metaphors of hope' embedded in the quality of Bahá'í law, the Kitáb-i-Aqdas has been described as: the 'Unerring Balance'; the 'Straight Path'; the 'quickener of mankind'; the 'River of Mercy'; and the 'Arc of His Laws'. Bahá'u'lláh has further characterized the laws and ordinances of His Most Holy Book as: 'the breath of life unto all created things'; 'the highest means for the maintenance of order in the world and the security of its peoples'; 'the lamps of His wisdom and loving- providence'; 'the keys of His mercy to His creatures'; 'the proof of the All-Merciful unto all who are in the heaven and all who are on earth'; and the 'weightiest testimony unto all people'.[38]

Such forceful descriptions of religious law for this age of human unification, from the Pen of the Holy Lawgiver Himself, manifest the mercy of God in rendering these transcendental concepts into an accessible form, in light of the inadequacies of human language to convey fully the power and beauty of revelation. Thus, metaphorical symbolism has been employed to endow the deep, powerful, poetic and creative words of 'veiled allusions' with new and exhilarating meanings.

Bahá'u'lláh, revealing concepts about the nature of divine law that are novel and stirring, has declared: 'By God! Such is the majesty of what hath been revealed therein, and so tremendous the revelation of its veiled allusions that the loins of utterance shake when attempting their description.'[39]

'the choice wine'

These 'veiled allusions' simplify complex ideas and carry them in a burst of insight to the heart. They nourish the mind and soul with vistas of truth. They educate in a flash of vision and raise the cultural level of believers. They convey deep impressions about the organic and teleologic intent of God's new laws for humanity.[40]

Despite the inherent limitations of language, symbolism remains the primary tool for the communication of divine teachings: it is a necessary means for conveying spiritual truth; a conveyor of concrete expression to intangible truths; a transitional device for bridging the gap between the spiritual and material world; a tool for facilitating spiritual transformation by evoking a transcendental experience. For example, `Abdu'l-Bahá singles out the pillar of fire appearing to Moses and the dove lighting upon Jesus as didactic symbolic devices.[41] His explanation affirms the traditional operation of the symbol in religion as being intrinsic to the very nature of language itself, particularly the highly metaphorical spiritual language of the heart.[42]

Although holy laws themselves are generally expressed in clear and unambiguous terms, symbolic language is employed in the holy scriptures to express the transformative and spiritualizing nature of divine law as a whole. In revealing the meanings of the verses of Jesus concerning the signs of His coming, Bahá'u'lláh discloses that by the terms 'heaven', 'sun', 'moon', 'stars', and 'clouds' is meant, 'in one sense', respectively, The Divine Lawgivers, 'Who rise from the dayspring of ancient glory, and fill the world with a liberal effusion of grace from on high'. The terms also mean 'such laws and teachings as have been established and proclaimed in every Dispensation', 'the annulment of laws firmly established by divine Revelation, all of which, in symbolic language, have been foreshadowed by the Manifestation of God', and 'the abrogation of former Dispensations, the repeal of rituals and customs current amongst men'.[43]

The following is perhaps the central metaphor, a striking and poignant example of Bahá'u'lláh's use of language in relation to His law: 'Think not that we have revealed unto you a mere code of laws. Nay, rather, We have unsealed the choice wine with the fingers of might and power.'[44]

Shoghi Effendi has written: 'The wine mentioned in the Tablets has undoubtedly a spiritual meaning . . . We see it thus used by the Persian poets such as Saadi and Umar Khayam and Hafiz to mean that element which nears man to his divine beloved, which makes him forget his material self so as better to seek his spiritual desires.'[45]

Bahá'u'lláh has revealed in *The Hidden Words*:

> Turn not away thine eyes from the matchless wine of the immortal Beloved, and open them not to foul and mortal dregs. Take from the hands of the divine Cup-bearer the chalice of immortal life, that all wisdom may be thine, and that thou mayest hearken unto the mystic voice calling from the realm of the invisible.[46]

Elsewhere, He identifies the heavenly substance as:

> that wine which intensifieth man's love for God, for His Chosen Ones and for His loved ones, and igniteth in the hearts the fire of God and love for Him, and glorification and praise of Him. So potent is this wine that a drop thereof will attract him . . . to attain the presence of God . . . a wine that blotteth out from the hearts of the true lovers all suggestions of limitation, establisheth the truth of the signs of His oneness and divine unity, and leadeth them to the Tabernacle of the Well-Beloved . . . We meant by this Wine, the River of God, and His favour, the fountain of His living waters, and the Mystic Wine and its divine grace . . .[47]

What moving symbolism, then, in light of these clarifications to equate the law of God with choice wine! Bahá'u'lláh's poetic choice of words suggests that Bahá'í law is a divine instrument for drawing humankind to the Beloved; obtaining spiritual desires; harkening unto the voice of God; igniting the fire of the love of God, glorification and praise of Him; intensifying love for God; attaining wisdom; blotting out from the heart all suggestions of limitation; and leading humankind to the tabernacle of the Well-Beloved.

The blessed verse suggests the inebriating effect of God's law in the day of human maturity, in which we may drink our fill of the heavenly elixir, yet retain our balance. Might the use of the term 'choice wine' also suggest that this precious gift will invigorate humanity to such an extent that the full potential will emerge from human reality, and that the law of God must assist in the ascent to our highest station? Perhaps it also represents that we are to internalize the divine law within our hearts with such vigour, consistent with the capacity of an adult stage, that the thought of anything but obedience to the good pleasure of God would be obliterated. Might not this also be the 'choice wine' that Jesus 'unveiled' at the marriage feast in Canna, which prompted the startled steward of the feast to demand of the puzzled bridegroom: 'Why have you saved the best wine for last?'[48]

The symbol of wine might also suggest a transformation to a spiritual state of intoxication with the sweetness of the law of God. In reference to the verse 'We have unsealed the choice wine', the following has considerable merit:

> Bahá'u'lláh's use of symbol of the unsealing of 'the choice wine', while suggesting the milder and more pleasant effects of intoxication, points to the ecstatic effect produced upon all creation by the unveiling of His divine laws. Also implicit in Bahá'u'lláh's image of the choice wine is the idea of the absorption of divine laws by the believer. The believer is to imbibe, so to speak, into his spiritual being the divine laws with the same relish that the experienced connoisseur quaffs the wine. Just as the choicest wine has been well aged in oak casks, Bahá'u'lláh's symbol indicates that the wine of His revelation unseals the flavour of the heady wisdom of the generations. Moreover, as some may view wine as nourishment for the body, Bahá'u'lláh uses the symbol of the choice wine to suggest nourishment for the soul and spiritual life.[49]

'expressive of the incomparable greatness of Bahá'u'lláh'
Bahá'í law is not merely a code of rules. It incorporates a divine process, an enterprise in which standards have meaning in the context of Bahá'u'lláh's station as the Supreme Manifestation of God, the intensity of His Revelation, His prescribed mission to establish the organic unity of peoples and nations. This process has included the promulgation of values and principles, such as justice, and the oneness of

humankind. It also consists of ways of thought, the integration of a pre-ordained, evolving plan for establishing a 'Divine Economy', the ordaining of institutions, procedures and modes of human governance, including the election and appointment of specialized servants. Also the enabling function of law of facilitating voluntary arrangements is significantly endorsed in Bahá'í law.

Such a broad concept of Bahá'í law is required in order to explore its relations to divine commands and prohibitions from earlier ages, as well as to current political, economic and social institutions, values and concepts. `Abdu'l-Bahá presents the following framework:

> the Law of God is divided into two parts. One is the fundamental basis which comprises all spiritual things— that is to say, it refers to the spiritual virtues and divine qualities; this does not change or alter: it is the Holy of Holies, which is the essence of the Law of Adam, Noah, Abraham, Moses, Christ, Muhammad, the Báb, and Bahá'u'lláh, and which lasts and is established in all the prophetic cycles. It will never be abrogated, for it is spiritual and not material truth; it is faith, knowledge, certitude, justice, piety, righteousness, trustworthiness, love of God, benevolence, purity, detachment, humility, meekness, patience and constancy. It shows mercy to the poor, defends the oppressed, gives to the wretched and uplifts the fallen. . . .

The second part of the religion of God, which refers to the material world, and which comprises fasting, prayer, forms of worship, marriage and divorce, the abolition of slavery, legal processes, transactions, indemnities for murder, violence, theft and injuries—this part of the Law of God, which refers to material things, is modified and altered in each prophetic cycle in accordance with the necessities of the times.[50]

While the spiritual laws (consisting of devotional precepts and ordinances concerning praise of God and fostering the spiritual development of the individual) indicate the grandeur of Bahá'u'lláh's station, the social laws contain the essence of a world order, including a legal order. These deepen our appreciation for basic social values such as order, liberty, and the instiution of the family, and appear to demonstrate more fully the greatness of the Bahá'í Revelation.

The second category includes those laws which secure justice; resolve actual and potential social conflicts or 'difference';[51] order society;[52] facilitate social intercourse;[53] regulate social relations;[54] protect basic freedoms;[55] establish institutions;[56] reinforce and protect the family as one of the most vital institutions in society;[57] establish procedures for the resolution of conflict;[58] and provide for the use of criminal law for protection and preservation of society.[59]

As it is beyond human capacity to fathom the essence of the station of the Manifestation of God, symbolism has also been utilized in exploring the meaning of divine law itself, as well as the rank and station of the laws of Bahá'u'lláh. When Moses went up Mount Sinai to receive the laws, which had been 'written with the finger of God', 'the glory of the Lord' covered the mountain.[60] 'And the sight of the glory of the Lord was like devouring fire on the top of the mount'.[61] When the great Lawgiver descended with the commandments, His face shone with such splendour that His followers were afraid to draw near. They had never seen the Prophet's face shining with the 'glory of the Lord'. Nevertheless, in this luminous state, Moses summoned them nigh and presented them with all that God had commanded. But, curiously, after he had given the laws, Moses put a veil on his face so that the people might look up at Him. Only when He went out to receive additional laws from the Almighty did He remove the veil.

Why should Moses, the personification of the Law in His Age, be portrayed wearing a mask? Does it mean that divine law is ultimately veiled from true understanding? Does it suggest that Moses had been given the laws in an age of immaturity, when the true meaning and purpose of religion and law were yet hidden? Does it mean that the fullness of divine law, or the capacity to understand or obey it, are limited until the appearance of the Supreme Manifestation of God? Perhaps the time for the full unveiling of the law of God before the peoples of the world has arrived with the Supreme Lawgiver, Bahá'u'lláh, the Fountain of the Most Great Justice. Is the promulgation of the Kitáb-i-Aqdas the lifting of the veil that Moses wore? In His proclamation of His Mission, Bahá'u'lláh significantly declares: 'My face hath come forth from the veils'.[62]

Of that luminous countenance, Professor E. G. Browne has written, 'The face of Him on Whom I gazed, I can never forget, though I cannot describe it. Those piercing eyes seemed to read one's very soul; power and authority sat on that ample brow.'[63]

Shaykh Hasan-i-Zunúzí, whom Siyyid Kázim had told that 'in the days to come yours shall be the inestimable joy of beholding 'what eye hath seen not, ear heard not, nor any heart conceived',[64] has left his account of what it means to have looked upon the unveiled face of the Lawgiver. Before relating Zunúzí's experience, we may recall the Báb's instructions to His disciple:

> You should proceed to Karbila and should abide in that holy city, inasmuch as you are destined to behold, with your own eyes, the beauteous countenance of the promised Husayn. As you gaze upon that radiant face, do also remember Me. Convey to Him the expression of my loving devotion. Verily I say, I have entrusted you with a great mission. Beware lest your heart grow faint, lest you forget the glory with which I have invested you.'[65]

In *The Dawn-Breakers* we read Shaykh Hasan's account:

while I was passing by the gate of the inner courtyard of the Shrine of the Imám Husayn, my eyes, for the first time, fell upon Bahá'u'lláh. What shall I recount regarding the countenance which I beheld! The beauty of that face, those exquisite features which no pen or brush dare describe, His penetrating glance, His kindly face, the majesty of His bearing, the sweetness of His smile, the luxuriance of His jet-black flowing locks, left an indelible impression upon my soul. I was then an old man, bowed with age. How lovingly he advanced towards me! He took me by the hand and, in a tone which at once betrayed power and beauty, addressed me in these words: 'This very day I have purposed to make you known as a Bábí throughout Karbila.' Still holding my hand in His, He continued to converse with me. He walked with me all along the market-street, and in the end He said: 'Praise be to God that you have remained in Karbila, and have beheld with your own eyes the countenance of the promised Husayn.' I recalled instantly the promise which had been given me by the Báb.[66]

I have discussed the veiling of Moses' face in order to stimulate thinking about the incomparable greatness of Bahá'u'lláh's laws. The great Bahá'í scholar Mírzá Abu'l-Fadl states that Bahá'u'lláh's characterizations of the properties and benefits of divine law have never been equalled in mankind's spiritual history, that Bahá'u'lláh has enacted laws and regulations concerning every point or subject referring to the preservation of society and the perfecting of human virtues; greater laws than which cannot be imagined by the possessors of intelligence. . . . It is only through such laws that the union and harmony among nations . . . can be effected; for, in enacting laws upon every subject, He has taken two points into consideration. First, that obeying and carrying them into practice may be possible for all peoples, notwithstanding the difference of their countries. Second, that they may not excite selfish prejudices and fanaticism. Through these laws, the breezes of ideal mercy and compassion will blow through hearts and souls, and the light of real humanity will shine forth from all breasts. Thus, through the assistance of God, the spirit of disunion, discord and hostility which divide nations, will be removed, and all the earth will be considered as one paradise and one home.[67]

Motive clauses

A further indication of the greatness of Bahá'u'lláh's Revelation and the rank of His laws involves the uncertain use of so called 'motive clauses'. Although both the Gospel and the Qur'án have verses in which believers are admonished to obey the commandments, the Old Testament contains a proliferation of such clauses, which are intended to motivate believers to follow specific commandments.

Motive clauses are phrases directly linked with a particular law that commends the specific law to the addressee. They are called 'motive clauses' because they attempt to incline the believer to perform the instruction being given, and generally serve a didactic function. They are usually uttered in the same breath as the laws and are not merely communicated as subsequent hortatory attachments. They may provide a short explanation of the purpose or policy of the law, promise a reward for obedience or extol the intent for keeping the law. They are frequently attached to unenforceable laws, rather than enforceable precepts. However, the enforceable laws on adultery and seduction in Deuteronomy have motive clauses.[68] Some of these clauses provide the promise of general material well-being and prosperity.

For example, the sage in Proverbs appeals to his disciple thus: 'Hear my son, thy father's instruction and reject not thy mother's teaching; for they are a fair garland for thy head and pendants for thy neck'.[69]

Often these clauses are introduced by the phrase 'in order that': 'A full and just weight thou shalt have, a full and just measure thou shalt have; in order that thy days may be prolonged';[70] 'Justice, Justice thou shalt follow in order that thou mayest live and inherit the land';[71] 'And when he [the King] sits on the throne of his kingdom, he shall write for himself in a book a copy of this law . . . and he shall read in it . . . keeping all the words of this law . . . that his heart may not be lifted up above his brethren, and that he may not turn aside from the commandments . . . so that he may continue long in his kingdom'.[72]

The reward of obedience is often stated as an appeal: 'My son, do not forget my teachings, but let thine heart keep my commandments; for length of days and years of life and abundant welfare will they give thee.'[73]

Thorough and comprehensive explorations of the use of motive clauses, or more general admonitions, in divine law is only one of the possible ways Bahá'í scholars might show how Bahá'í is similar to, or distinct from divinely revealed standards of old. The following verses suggest a pattern:

> Lay not upon your souls that which will weary them and weigh them down, but rather what will lighten and uplift them, so that they may soar on the wings of the Divine verses towards the Dawning-place of His manifest signs; this will draw you nearer to God, did ye but comprehend.[74]

> Unto everyone hath been enjoined the writing of a will. The testator should head this document with the adornment of the Most Great Name, bear witness therein unto the oneness of God . . . and make mention, as he may wish, of that which is praiseworthy, so that it may be a testimony for him in the kingdoms of Revelation and Creation and a treasure with his Lord, the Supreme Protector, the Faithful.[75]

It is forbidden you to trade in slaves, be they men or women. It is not for him who is himself a servant to buy another of God's servants, and this hath been prohibited in His Holy Tablet. Thus, by His mercy, hath the commandment been recorded by the Pen of justice. Let no man exalt himself above another; all are but bondslaves before the Lord, and all exemplify the truth that there is none other God but Him.[76]

Cling, O ye people of Bahá, to the cord of servitude unto God, the True One, for thereby your stations shall be made manifest, your names written and preserved, your ranks raised and your memory exalted in the Preserved Tablet.[77]

What is conspicuous in the Bahá'í Writings, however, are a number of verses conveying the blessings vouchsafed by the law. For example, in the Kitáb-i-Aqdas itself it is revealed: 'Blessed is he who observeth that whereunto he hath been bidden by Him Who ruleth over all mankind';[78] 'Blessed, then, be those who do Our bidding';[79] 'Blessed the man that observeth that whereunto he was bidden, and woe betide the negligent.'[80] And: 'Happy are they who are endued with true wisdom and understanding, who see and perceive, who read and understand, and who observe that which God hath revealed in the Holy Books of old, and in this incomparable and wondrous Tablet';[81] 'Observe My commandments, for the love of My beauty';[82] 'Happy is the lover that hath inhaled the divine fragrance of his Best-Beloved from these words, laden with the perfume of a grace which no tongue can describe. By My life! He who hath drunk the choice wine of fairness from the hands of My bountiful favour will circle around My commandments that shine above the Dayspring of My creation.'[83] And: 'Well is it with him who hath adorned himself with the vesture of seemly conduct and a praisewor-thy character. He is assuredly reckoned with those who aid their Lord through distinctive and outstanding deeds';[84] 'Well is it with him who hath quaffed the Mystic Wine of everlast-ing life from the utterance of His merciful Lord in My Name —a Name through which every lofty and majestic mountain hath been reduced to dust.'[85]

'a vast process . . . Exerting an increasingly powerful transformative effect on peoples and nations'

Our civilization is strikingly distinguished from that of earlier ages by what may be described as its essentially secular character. Religion and divine law, which were once regarded as the very foundation of the common life of society, are looked upon today as a matter left to individual choice or even caprice. These two potent instruments for the peace and tranquillity of a disordered world community, characterized increasingly by fundamental divisions of race, class, the sexes and the generations, and where bonds of faith, kinship and of land have eroded, are generally regarded as factors which do not, or at least ought not to, enter into political arrangements or affect the freedom of individual or State intercourse. While the statesman or student of affairs may well allow for religious affinities as a factor in his calculations, it is scarcely regarded as permissible to appeal to them in justification of public action. With the breakdown of order, confidence has waned in law as a way of protecting the individual and national communities against corrupting social, economic and political forces.

Notwithstanding, it is not surprising to a Bahá'í that in an age where 'conceptions of duty . . . are distorted',[86] Bahá'u'lláh has imposed spiritual and legal duties. As `Abdu'l-Bahá has explained, these duties are not the result of the imposition of power, which has scarred the landscape of human relations, but of truth, reality and justice.[87] The view of the Bahá'í Faith is that law is not separated from other processes of social control. Rather, it is a vast process involving peoples and nations. The part of the process dealing with nations implies quite serious legal policies and consequences.

Of course, the concepts of responsibility and duty are linked with the idea of obedience. The forces of obligation or duty and obedience are well-known instruments in legal science. Nevertheless, obedience to law is generally acknowledged as a duty only by those who truly recognize the authority of the law, or the right of the lawmaker to command. People and nations who obey law from fear of punishment alone are said to act not from duty but from expediency.

In other words, they calculate the risks and consequences, rather than being inspired by love for the lawmaker and a sense of righteousness.[88]

It may not be as clear, however, that the Bahá'í Writings contain a host of fundamental or 'constitutional' duty-creating principles for a federated world commonwealth of States, which may gradually evolve into binding State responsibilities and duties.[89] This is an extremely significant aspect of Bahá'í law. This prospect may be related to Bahá'u'lláh's censure of the rulers of His time for their 'failure in duty' to Him,[90] and His warnings: 'Be not forgetful of the law of God in whatever thou desirest to achieve, now or in the days to come';[91] 'Observe, O King, . . . the precepts of God, and walk not in the paths of the oppressor.'[92] It appears also to be related to a return to the Western legal tradition of belief in the existence of a body of law—once ceded to divine law, then natural law, and more recently human rights—which is beyond the law of the highest political authority.

The evolving process of State responsibility is clearly related to Shoghi Effendi's vision of a world order with an international tribunal possessing binding jurisdiction, and in which there is a duty on States to faithfully obey and execute international law and to implement Bahá'u'lláh's system of collective security. Clearly, the development of broad legal policies about State responsibility are at stake, in view of the principle of State sovereignty, based on human and municipal analogies, and the lingering debate over whether international can be said to be 'law', in the absence of true coercive power in all instances to compel obedience or punish disobedience.

Martha Schweitz has shown that the Kitáb-i-Aqdas incorporates some of the most basic of the 'general principles of laws recognized by civilized nations' and that:

> The beauty of the embryonic system of *The Kitáb-i-Aqdas* is that the principles which set the context for its further development, interpretation and application are explicit, and often elaborated in considerable detail in *The Kitáb-i-Aqdas* and in other Bahá'í writings. . . . These principles are universal, comprehensive and immutable.'[93]

However, questions about duties and responsibilities are at the heart of most political debates, i.e. the responsible use of force against aggression and oppression, the morality of intervention in the affairs of other nations in order to relieve human suffering, the protection of the environment etc. Each of these questions, and many others, hinges on the idea of responsibility, and the exercise of power by human agents of governmental institutions, whose conduct can be guided by law and principles. In an age marked by the radical extension of human power through technology, myriad forms of injustices and increasing moral division and conflict, it is not surprising that the idea of responsibility should be so central to moral reflection and debate.

The Writings of the Bahá'í Faith present new categories of duties and principles, alongside the traditional duties pertaining to individuals and corporate bodies, great and small, up to the nation State. Bahá'u'lláh's prescripts for nations are found in His Book of Laws (which 'constitute the kernel of a vast range of law that will arise in centuries to come'),[94] His letters to the kings and rulers of the world, and other Tablets.

What appears to be some of the responsibilities and duties of States that are unfolding within the process of Bahá'í law are set out below.

The Bahá'í Writings admonish government officials to exercise their powers in good faith. For example, Bahá'u'lláh directs the leaders: 'be thou of them that act uprightly';[95] 'Put thy whole confidence in the grace of God thy Lord. Let Him be thy trust in whatever thou doest, and be of them that have submitted themselves to His Will. Let Him be thy helper and enrich thyself with His treasure, for with Him are the treasuries of the heavens and of the earth';[96] 'strive thou to rule with equity among men';[97] 'Be anxiously concerned with the needs of the age ye live in, and centre your deliberations on its exigencies and requirements';[98] 'arise to enforce the law of God . . . that thou mayest be of those who are firmly established in His law.'[99]

The duty of persons in fiduciary positions—such as governmental officials— not to allow their personal interests to conflict with their official duties is also embedded in

Bahá'í law: 'Overstep not the bounds of moderation, and deal justly with them that serve thee. Bestow upon them according to their needs, and not to the extent that will enable them to lay up riches for themselves, to deck their persons, to embellish their homes, to acquire the things that are of no benefit unto them, and to be numbered with the extravagant.'[100] 'Beware lest thou aggrandize thy ministers at the expense of thy subjects';[101] 'Beware lest thou appropriate unto thyself the things of the world and the riches thereof';[102] 'let your concern be only for that which profiteth mankind, and bettereth the condition thereof, if ye be of them that scan heedfully.'[103]

Finally, it appears that the seeds of the duty to exercise care, skill, and diligence lie in Bahá'u'lláh's messages to the kings: 'Beware . . . that thou not gather around thee such ministers as follow the desires of a corrupt inclination';[104] 'repose not thy confidence in ministers unworthy of thy trust . . . entrust them not with thine affairs';[105] 'Hold firmly within the grasp of thy might, the reins of the affairs of the people, and examine in person whatever pertaineth unto them';[106] 'Allow not the abject to rule over and dominate them who are noble and worthy of honour, and suffer not the high-minded to be at the mercy of the contemptible and worthless';[107] 'Inquire into their affairs [the poor] and ascertain, every year, nay every month, their condition, and be not of them who are careless of their duty';[108] 'Have a care not to entrust thine affairs of state entirely into another's hands. None can discharge thy functions better than thine own self.'[109]

95

Notes & references

1. The Kitáb-i-Aqdas, The Most Holy Book, the Mother Book, the Book of Laws of the Bahá'í Faith, was revealed in `Akká in 1873. Numbers not preceded by 'p.', refer to numbered paragraphs in the published text of the Kitáb-i-Aqdas.

2. Letter from the Universal House of Justice to the Bahá'ís of the world, 5 March 1993, *The Holy Year 1992-1993* (Riviera Beach, Fla: Palabra Publications, 1993), p. 46.

3. Ibid., p. 45.

4. `Abdu'l-Bahá, *Some Answered Questions*, comp. and trans. Laura Clifford Barney, 1st pocket size ed. (Wilmette, Ill: Bahá'í Publishing Trust, 1984), p. 158.

5. Ibid.

6. Ibid., p. 159.

7. `Abdu'l-Bahá, *The Secret of Divine Civilization*, trans. Marzieh Gail, 1st pocket size ed. (Wilmette, Ill: Bahá'í Publishing Trust, 1994), p. 46.

8. Ibid., p. 20.

9. Idem, *Some Answered Questions*, p. 173.

10. Ibid, pp. 48-9, 93-6, 159.

11. Idem, *The Secret of Divine Civilization*, p. 35.

12. Ibid., p. 82.

13. Noel Coulson, *Conflicts and Tensions In Islamic Jurisprudence* (Chicago: University of Chicago Press, 1969), p. 91.

14. Bahá'u'lláh, *The Kitáb-i-Aqdas: The Most Holy Book*, rev. ed. (London: Bahá'í Publishing Trust, 1993), pp. 4, 6-7, 91.

15. Ibid., 4.

16. Ibid., 4-12, 22, 26, 47, 53, 81-82, 132, 143, 183, 165; Idem, *Tablets of Bahá'u'lláh revealed after the Kitáb-i-Aqdas*, comp. Research Department of the Universal House of Justice, trans. Habib Taherzadeh with the assistance of a Committee at the Bahá'í World Centre, 1st US hardcover ed. (Wilmette, Ill: Bahá'í Publishing Trust, 1993), pp. 132,

120. On the employment of divine law to demonstrate the authority of the Manifestation of God, see idem, *Kitáb-i-Íqán: The Book of Certitude*, trans. Shoghi Effendi, 3rd ed. (London: Bahá'í Publishing Trust, 1982), pp. 18, 20, 27, 62, 71-74, 84, 107.

17. Shoghi Effendi, *Principles of Bahá'í Administration*, 4th ed. (London: Bahá'í Publishing Trust, 1976), p. 1.

18. `Abdu'l-Bahá, *The Secret of Divine Civilization*, p. 85.

19. Bahá'u'lláh, *Gleanings from the Writings of Bahá'u'lláh*, comp. and trans. Shoghi Effendi, rev. ed. (London: Bahá'í Publishing Trust, 1978), LXXXVIII, p. 174.

20. `Abdu'l-Bahá, *The Secret of Divine Civilization*, p. 27.

21. Bahá'u'lláh, *Tablets*, p. 126.

22. Idem, Kitáb-i-Aqdas, 1, 29, 75, 121, 155, pp. 121, 145-162, 159-161; also: 'The Laws of God are not imposition of will or of power or of pleasure, but the resolution of truth, reason and justice' `Abdu'l-Bahá, *Paris Talks: Addresses Given by `Abdu'l-Bahá in 1911*, 12th rev. ed. (London: Bahá'í Publishing Trust, 1995), 47:1, p. 160.

23. Bahá'u'lláh, *Gleanings*, CXXXIII, pp. 288-9.

24. Idem, Kitáb-i-Aqdas, 98.

25. Ibid., 185, 186.

26. Ibid., 96.

27. Ibid., 2.

28. Idem, *Tablets*, pp. 50, 93.

29. Idem, Kitáb-i-Aqdas, 88.

30. `Abdu'l-Bahá, *The Secret of Divine Civilization*, p. 83.

31. Ibid., p. 60.

32. Bahá'u'lláh, Kitáb-i-Aqdas, 45.

33. Ibid., 59.

34. Ibid., 125.

35. Ibid., 65.

36. Ibid., p. 2.

37. Idem, *Tablets*, pp. 129-30.

38. Shoghi Effendi, *God Passes By*, rev. ed. (Wilmette, Ill: Bahá'í Publishing Trust, 1979), pp. 215-16.

39. Bahá'u'lláh, Kitáb-i-Aqdas, p. 16.

40. See Earl R. MacCormac, *Metaphor and Myth in Science and Religion* (Durham: Duke University Press, 1976), pp. 39, 72.

41. `Abdu'l-Bahá, *Some Answered Questions*, p. 85.

42. J. A. McLean observes that, 'the symbol in revelation-language is a vehicle for the power of the Holy Spirit. The individual must be open, however, to the possibility of symbol, must be willing to participate in and be sensitive to the power of the images being unveiled, to allow himself to be transported by them. Otherwise, the symbol with its poetic expressions will be looked upon only as on unnecessary distraction. It is precisely because the symbol is liable to evoke deep and meaningful spiritual experiences that it has had such recurring and enduring power in the history of religion.' *Dimensions in Spirituality* (Oxford: George Ronald, 1994), p. 206.

43. Bahá'u'lláh, *Kitáb-i-Íqán*, pp. 24, 33, 38, 41, 71.

44. Idem, Kitáb-i-Aqdas, 5.

45. From a letter written on behalf of Shoghi Effendi dated 4 November 1926, in *Prohibition of Intoxicating Drinks*, comp. Research Department of the Universal House of Justice (Lagos: Publishing Committee of the National Spiritual Assembly of the Bahá'ís of Nigeria, 1982), p. 7.

46. Bahá'u'lláh, *The Hidden Words*, trans. Shoghi Effendi with the assistance of some English friends (London: Nightingale Books, 1992), p. 77.

47. From a letter written on behalf of Shoghi Effendi dated 4 November 1926, included in *Prohibition*, p. 2.

48. John 2:10.

49. McLean, op. cit., p. 210.

50. `Abdu'l-Bahá, *Some Answered Questions*, p. 47-48.

51. Bahá'u'lláh, Kitáb-i-Aqdas, 53.

52. Ibid., 2, 4, 7, 16, 33, 39, 44, 45, 48, 64, 71, 73, 97, 113, 138, 144, 155, 156.

53. Ibid., 31, 57, 58, 75, 76, 106, 119, 147, 155, 156.

54. Ibid., 2, 13, 19.

55. Ibid., 9, 46, 51, 123.

56. Ibid., 39.

57. Ibid., 20, 29, 63-66, 68, 69, 70, 113.

58. Ibid., 42, 52, 56, 62.

59. Ibid., 19, 45, 49, 52, 56, 62, 73, 148, 155, 188, 190.

60. Exod. 24:16.

61. Ibid., 24:17.

62. Bahá'u'lláh, *The Proclamation of Bahá'u'lláh to the Kings and Leaders of the World* (Haifa: Bahá'í World Centre, 1973), p. 8.

63. Shoghi Effendi, *God Passes By*, p. 194.

64. Nabíl-A'zám, *The Dawn-Breakers: Nabíl's Narrative of the Early Days of the Bahá'í Revelation*, translated from the original Persian by Shoghi Effendi (London: Bahá'í Publishing Trust, 1932), p. 22.

65. Ibid., p. 24.

66. Ibid., pp. 24-5

67. Mírzá Abu'l-Fadl Gulpaygání, *The Bahá'í Proofs (Hujaja'l-Bahíyyih) and A Short Sketch of the History and Lives of the Leaders of This Religion*, trans. Ali-Kuli Khan (Ishti'al Ibn-i-Kalántar), facsimile of 1929 ed. (Wilmette: Bahá'í Publishing Trust, 1983), p. 91.

68. Deut. 22.

69. Prov. 1:8-9.

70. Deut. 25.15.

71. Ibid., 6:20.

72. Ibid., 17:18-20.

73. Prov. 3:1-2.

74. Bahá'u'lláh, Kitáb-i-Aqdas, 149.

75. Ibid., 109.

76. Ibid., 72.

77. Ibid., 120.

78. Ibid., 8.

79. Ibid., 108.

80. Ibid., 171.

81. Ibid., 'Questions and Answers', 106.

82. Ibid., 4.

83. Ibid.

84. Ibid., 150.

85. Ibid., 4, 7, 8, 108, 138, 147, 150, 171.

86. Shoghi Effendi, *The World Order of Bahá'u'lláh: Selected Letters*, 2nd rev. ed. (Wilmette, Ill: Bahá'í Publishing Trust, 1974), p. 187.

87. `Abdu'l-Bahá, *Paris Talks*, 47, p. 160.

88. The love of God is the motive for observance of divine law. See Bahá'u'lláh, Kitáb-i-Aqdas, 4, 162-3.

89. See Martha Schweitz, 'The Kitáb-i-Aqdas: Bahá'í Law, Legitimacy and World Order', in *The Journal of Bahá'í Studies*, vol. 6, no. 1, March-June 1994, p. 42.

90. Bahá'u'lláh, *Gleanings*, LXVI, p. 130.

91. Ibid., CXIV, p. 239.

92. Ibid., p. 233.

93. Schweitz, op. cit., p. 43.

94. Bahá'u'lláh, Kitáb-i-Aqdas, p. 4. Along the same line, it has been noted, 'The World Order of Bahá'u'lláh, however, is still growing in its embryonic form. In the fullness of time it will be born and will usher in an age the glories of which we in this day cannot fully visualize, an age in which the teachings of Bahá'u'lláh will guide and govern the life of man on this planet. Then and only then will the wisdom and significance of all the laws of the Kitáb-i-Aqdas become manifest, their

relevance to the needs of the age become apparent and the application become a vital necessity.' Adib Taherzadeh, *The Revelation of Bahá'u'lláh: `Akká, The Early Years 1868-77*, vol. 3 (Oxford: George Ronald, 1983), p. 281.

95. Bahá'u'lláh, *Proclamation*, p. 47.
96. Ibid., p. 49.
97. Ibid., p. 50.
98. Ibid., p. 116.
99. Ibid., p. 49.
100. Ibid., p. 50.
101. Ibid.
102. Ibid., p. 67.
103. Ibid.
104. Ibid., p. 47.
105. Ibid., p. 48.
106. Ibid.
107. Ibid., p. 50.
108. Ibid., p. 51.
109. Ibid.

HOW CLOSE ARE WE TO THE LESSER PEACE?

Wendi Momen

'What's your view of all these London changes, Forsyte? You remember the peg-top trouser, and the crinoline—Leech in his prime . . .'

'It's all on the surface,' said Soames.

'On the surface? I sometimes have that feeling. But there is a real change. It's the difference between the Austen and Trollope novels and these modern fellows. There are no parishes left. Classes? Yes, but divided by man, not by God, as in Trollope's day.'

Soames sniffed. The chap was always putting things in that sort of way!

'At the rate we're going, they'll soon not be divided at all,' he said.

'I think you're wrong there, Forsyte. I should never be surprised to see the horse come back.'

'The horse,' muttered Soames; 'what's he got to do with it?'

'What we must look for,' said Sir Lawrence, swinging his cane, 'is the millennium. Then we shall soon be developing individuality again. And the millennium's nearly here.'

'I don't in the least follow you,' said Soames.

'Education's free; women have the vote; even the workman has or soon will have his car; the slums are doomed . . .; amusement and news are in every home; the Liberal Party's up the spout, Free Trade's a moveable feast; sport's cheap and plentiful; dogma's got the knock; so has the General Strike; Boy Scouts are increasing rapidly; dress is comfortable; and hair is short—it's all millennial.'

'What's all that got to do with the horse?'

'A symbol, my dear Forsyte. It's impossible to standardize or socialize a horse. We're beginning to react against uniformity. A little more millennium and we shall soon be cultivating our souls and driving tandem again.'[1]

* * *

B AHÁ'ÍS LOOK FORWARD to the end of the millennium with the same sense of expectation that has characterized those anticipating the return of Christ and the establishment of the Kingdom of God on earth. As this date draws nearer, speculation and excitement increases.

But what do we expect to find at the end of the millennium? Since the Bahá'í literature and the talks of `Abdu'l-Bahá abound with references to the Lesser Peace—a peace which is associated with the twentieth century—many, perhaps most, Bahá'ís believe that somehow, despite present world tensions, the Lesser Peace will be established, at least in some measure, by the end of the millennium.

A decade has passed since the Universal House of Justice released *The Promise of World Peace*, a document received by Bahá'ís with great enthusiasm, but perhaps little expectation of its effectiveness. A large number of Heads of State and lesser worthies received the statement with good grace, and a small number of governments responded favourably to its message. However, time moved on and the world's governments did not overtly take up the challenge it posed to convene the convocation of leaders. Changes have taken place in the international arena, of course, in the intervening years, changes which have inspired Bahá'ís to think positively of the possibility that the Lesser Peace—or some elements of it—might be established before the end of the century, a possibility which seemed, in reality, very remote in 1985. Indeed, certain of these changes—the crumbling of the Berlin Wall, heralding the apparent demolition of communism in most parts of the world, followed by the ending of the Cold War—have led some Bahá'ís to believe that the peace proclaimed by the Universal House of Justice to be 'inevitable' was indeed virtually here.

More recent events—in the former Yugoslavia, Rwanda and several of the Russian States—have blighted this possibility somewhat. The future does not look perhaps quite so bright as it did even three years ago. At the same time, the recurrence of right-wing extremism in Europe and North America has further dampened the zeal with which the advent of the Lesser Peace is proclaimed.

This paper examines various aspects of the Lesser Peace and its institutions, and attempts to chart progress towards its establishment through indicators found in the literature of the Bahá'í Faith.

What do we actually know about the Lesser Peace?

In 1931 Shoghi Effendi suggested that we know very little about the Lesser Peace:

> To claim to have grasped all the implications of Bahá'u'lláh's prodigious scheme for world-wide human solidarity, or to have fathomed its import, would be presumptuous on the part of even the declared support-ers of His Faith. To attempt to visualize it in all its possibilities, to estimate its future benefits, to picture its glory, would be premature at even so advanced a stage in the evolution of mankind.
>
> All we can reasonably venture to attempt is to strive to obtain a glimpse of the first streaks of the promised Dawn that must, in the fullness of time, chase away the gloom that has encircled humanity. All we can do is to point out, in their broadest outlines, what appear to us to be the guiding principles underlying the World Order of Bahá'u'lláh, as amplified and enunciated by `Abdu'l-Bahá . . .[2]

But Shoghi Effendi—and, after him, the Universal House of Justice—have picked out the basic elements of the Lesser Peace, which we will briefly rehearse here:

1) The Lesser Peace 'will initially be a political unity arrived at by decision of the governments of the various nations';[3]

2) This 'momentous and historic step' will involve the 'reconstruction of mankind, as the result of the universal recognition of its oneness and wholeness';[4]

3) This restructuring will require that 'some form of a world super-state' 'be evolved'[5] led by a world government;

4) The first step towards the creation of a true world government is, Shoghi Effendi says, 'the inevitable curtailment of unfettered national sovereignty'.[6] Those features of sovereignty which will need to be curtailed are similar to those curtailed among the federated member States of the United States: 'every claim to make war, certain rights to impose taxation and all rights to maintain armaments, except for the purposes of maintaining internal order within their respective dominions';[7]

5) 'Such a state will have to include within its orbit', Shoghi Effendi says, 'an international executive adequate to enforce supreme and unchallengeable authority on every recalcitrant member of the commonwealth; a world parliament whose members shall be elected by the people in their respective countries and whose election shall be confirmed by their respective governments; and a supreme tribunal whose

judgment will have a binding effect even in such cases where the parties concerned did not voluntarily agree to submit their case to its consideration';[8]

6) This world super-state will be 'backed by an International force';[9]

7) The nature of this super-state is to be a 'federal union';[10]

8) The system will work through the operation of collective security.[11]

9) The characteristics of the world society in which this super-state will operate have been described by Shoghi Effendi: 'all economic barriers will have been permanently demolished, the interdependence of Capital and Labour definitely recognized, the clamour of religious fanaticism and strife will have been forever stilled, the flame of racial animosity will have been finally extinguished, a single code of international law—the product of the considered judgment of the world's federated representatives—shall have as its sanction the instant and coercive intervention of the combined forces of the federated units . . . the fury of a capricious and militant nationalism will have been transmuted into an abiding consciousness of world citizenship'.[12]

10) The time frame within which the Lesser Peace is to be 'established' is said to be 'by the end of the century', and there are indications that this means the end of the twentieth century:[13] 'It [the Lesser Peace] will be established in this century. It will be universal in the twentieth century. All

nations will be forced into it.'[14]

11) Two events apparently must precede the establishment of the Lesser Peace: a convocation of the rulers of the world and some sort of world calamity.

There has been some clarification of the nature of some of the institutions of the Lesser Peace, since 1913, when, while on His Western journeys, 'Abdu'l-Bahá spoke about the Supreme Tribunal.[15]

There have also been more indications of when the Lesser Peace will come, and what it will look like when it arrives. For example, in 1954 Shoghi Effendi wrote of the development of the edifices on Mount Carmel, to be built along a 'far-flung arc', the 'ultimate completion' of which 'stupendous undertaking' would mark the 'culmination of the development of a world-wide divinely-appointed Administrative Order'. This would 'synchronize with two no less significant developments -- the establishment of the Lesser Peace and the evolution of Bahá'í national and local institutions'.[16]

The Universal House of Justice has charted humanity's progress towards the Lesser Peace, without adding much to the description of the institutions that will be developed or the kind of world that can be expected at that time. However it has defined the difference between the Lesser Peace—'when the unity of nations will be achieved'—and the Most Great Peace—'the spiritual as well as social and political unity of mankind'. It has also indicated that the Lesser Peace, once established, will develop in stages.[17]

Thus, we can anticipate in very general terms what the shape of the Lesser Peace will be, broadly how its institutions will be structured and the approximate time of its arrival.

Expectation of Bahá'ís about the Lesser Peace

Despite the above, theories abound among Bahá'ís as to what the Lesser Peace will be, when it will come, and how.

The 'Big Bang' Theory

Perhaps most prevalent is the view that might well be called 'big bang'. That is that the Lesser Peace will arrive suddenly, as the result of some enormous physical upheaval in the world. This is akin to the fundamentalist Christian view of the return of Christ on a cloud, where everyone in the world is expected to be able to see Christ returned at the same time.

Shoghi Effendi has indicated, particularly in the letters published in *The World Order of Bahá'u'lláh* and *Citadel of Faith*, that the establishment of the Lesser Peace must needs be preceded by a calamity. Numerous pilgrims' notes expand this position, although the notes themselves are, of course, unauthorized, and possibly inaccurate.

Those who hold the 'big bang' view cite passages from the Writings, and from the works of Shoghi Effendi:[18]

> The world is in travail, and its agitation waxeth day by day. Its face is turned towards waywardness and unbelief. Such shall be its plight, that to disclose it now

would not be meet and seemly. Its perversity will long continue. And when the appointed hour is come, there shall suddenly appear that which shall cause the limbs of mankind to quake. Then, and only then, will the Divine Standard be unfurled, and the Nightingale of Paradise warble its melody.[19]

The process of disintegration must inexorably continue, and its corrosive influence must penetrate deeper and deeper into the very core of a crumbling age. Much suffering will still be required ere the contending nations, creeds, classes and races of mankind are fused in the crucible of universal affliction, and are forged by the fires of a fierce ordeal into one organic commonwealth, one vast, unified, and harmoniously functioning system. Adversities unimaginably appalling, undreamed of crises and upheavals, war, famine, and pestilence, might well combine to engrave in the soul of an unheeding generation those truths and principles which it has disdained to recognize and follow. A paralysis more painful than any it has yet experienced must creep over and further afflict the fabric of a broken society ere it can be rebuilt and regenerated.[20]

Adversity, prolonged, worldwide, afflictive, allied to chaos and universal destruction, must needs convulse the nations, stir the conscience of the world, disillusion the masses, precipitate a radical change in the very conception of society, and coalesce ultimately the disjointed, the bleeding limbs of mankind into one body, single, organically united, and indivisible.

To the general character, the implications and features of this world commonwealth, destined to emerge, sooner or later, out of the carnage, agony, and havoc of this great world convulsion, I have already referred in my previous communications. Suffice it to say that this consummation will, by its very nature, be a gradual process, and must, as Bahá'u'lláh has Himself anticipated, lead at first to the establishment of that Lesser Peace which the nations of the earth, as yet unconscious of His Revelation and yet unwittingly enforcing the general principles which He has enunciated, will themselves establish.[21]

The Process Theory

Other Bahá'ís hold that the Lesser Peace is a process, with varying dates given for its beginning: the appearance of the Maid of Heaven to Bahá'u'lláh in the Siyáh-Chál, Bahá'u'lláh's call to the kings and rulers of His time, the revelation of the Tablets of the Divine Plan, the establishment of the League of Nations or, alternatively, the United Nations, and the release of *The Promise of World Peace*. The process theory draws on such works as Shoghi Effendi's statement to the American Bahá'ís in 1947:

Indeed if we would read aright the signs of the times, and appraise correctly the significances of contemporaneous events . . . we cannot fail to perceive the workings of two simultaneous processes, generated as far back as the concluding years of the Heroic Age of our Faith, each clearly defined, each distinctly separate, yet closely related and destined to culminate, in the fullness of time, in a single glorious consummation.

One of these processes is associated with the mission of the American Bahá'í Community, the other with the destiny of the American nation. The one serves directly the interests of the Administrative Order of the Faith of Bahá'u'lláh, the other promotes indirectly the institutions that are to be associated with the establishment of His World Order. The first process dates back to the revelation of those stupendous Tablets constituting the Charter of 'Abdu'l-Bahá's Divine Plan . . . It will be consummated through the emergence of the Bahá'í World Commonwealth in the Golden Age of the Bahá'í Dispensation.

The other process dates back to the outbreak of the first World War . . . It received its initial impetus through the formulation of President Wilson's Fourteen Points . . . It suffered its first setback through the dissociation of that republic from the newly born League of Nations . . . It acquired added momentum through the outbreak of the second World War . . . It was further reinforced through the declaration embodied in the Atlantic Charter . . . It assumed a definite outline through the birth of the United Nations at the San Francisco Conference. It acquired added significance through the choice of the City of the Covenant itself as the seat of the newly born organization . . . It must, however long and tortuous the way, lead, through a series of victories and reverses, to the political unification of the Eastern and Western Hemispheres, to the emergence of a world government and the establishment of the Lesser Peace . . . It must, in the end, culminate in the unfurling of the banner of the Most Great Peace, in the Golden Age of the Dispensation of Bahá'u'lláh.[22]

Proponents of this view suggest that the elements of the Lesser Peace are being built up gradually through a variety of international agreements, instruments and practices, and that the whole cluster of world summits that have taken place since the establishment of the United Nations in 1945 could be considered to be one long 'convocation'.

The 'the House will tell us' theory
Another view is that we will know when the Lesser Peace has arrived because the Universal House of Justice will tell us. Throughout the years the Universal House of Justice has given indications of where the world is in relation to predictions found in the Bahá'í Writings. For example, in 1967 we

find the Universal House of Justice saying that humanity had entered 'the dark heart of this age of transition'.[23] More recently it suggested 'that there are indications that the Lesser Peace cannot be too far distant'.[24]

Proponents of this view expect that one day, possibly soon, the Universal House of Justice will inform the Bahá'ís of the world that the Lesser Peace has finally arrived.

How close are we to the Lesser Peace?

Those who are natural compromisers will say that all these views are right in some ways. Drawing on elements from each of these views, then, it is possible to construct a list of indicators which, when placed against current world events, may help us determine how close we are to the Lesser Peace—not just in the sense of time but also in the sense of having fulfilled the conditions necessary for its establishment.[25]

Indicator 1: the convocation of world leaders
Bahá'u'lláh foresaw that,

> The time must come when the imperative necessity for the holding of a vast, an all-embracing assemblage of men will be universally realized. The rulers and kings of the earth must needs attend it, and, participating in its deliberations, must consider such ways and means as will lay the foundations of the world's Great Peace

amongst men. Such a peace demandeth that the Great
Powers should resolve, for the sake of the tranquillity of
the peoples of the earth, to be fully reconciled among
themselves.[26]

`Abdu'l-Bahá suggests that heads of government will call
the summit: 'A certain number of its (the world's) distinguished and high-minded sovereigns—the shining exemplars
of devotion and determination—shall, for the good and
happiness of all mankind, arise, with firm resolve and clear
vision, to establish the Cause of Universal Peace.'[27] The
features of this summit were established by `Abdu'l-Bahá:

They must make the Cause of Peace the object of
general consultation, and seek by every means in their
power to establish a Union of the nations of the world.
They must conclude a binding treaty and establish a
covenant, the provisions of which shall be sound,
inviolable and definite. They must proclaim it to all the
world and obtain for it the sanction of all the human
race. This supreme and noble undertaking—the real
source of the peace and well-being of all the
world—should be regarded as sacred by all that dwell on
earth. All the forces of humanity must be mobilized to
ensure the stability and permanence of this Most Great
Covenant.[28]

The Covenant establishing the world super-state must include certain provisions:

the limits and frontiers of each and every nation should be clearly fixed, the principles underlying the relations of governments towards one another definitely laid down, and all international agreements and obligations ascertained. In like manner, the size of the armaments of every government should be strictly limited, for if the preparations for war and the military forces of any nation should be allowed to increase, they will arouse the suspicion of others.[29]

The basis for action within the world super-state developed by the convocation and sustained by its Covenant is collective security. Bahá'u'lláh Himself stated: 'Should any king take up arms against another, all should unitedly arise and prevent him.'[30] And again, 'Be united, O kings of the earth, for thereby will the tempest of discord be stilled amongst you, and your peoples find rest. Should any one among you take up arms against another, rise ye all against him, for this is naught but manifest justice.'[31]

In 1985 the Universal House of Justice stated that this convocation was 'long overdue'.[32] Thus while it is tempting to consider the gathering in San Francisco fifty years ago to create the United Nations as the required convocation, it cannot be. Indeed, that gathering took place during the life of

Shoghi Effendi, who mentioned it[33] but never suggested that this was the convocation called for by Bahá'u'lláh.[34]

Clearly no single convocation has taken place that fulfils all the criteria set out by `Abdu'l-Bahá. However, as a decade has passed since the Universal House of Justice made this statement, it can be argued (and is by those who hold the 'process theory' to be true) that the recent round of development summits and conferences on population, human rights, the environment, human habitations and social development plus the possible forthcoming one on global governance together make up the convocation called for by Bahá'u'lláh.

The Universal House of Justice in its letter to the Bahá'ís introducing the document *The Prosperity of Humankind* in 1995, sees the recent round of conferences as 'capstones to the myriad activities taking place in different parts of the world involving a wide range of non-governmental organizations and networks in an urgent search for values, ideas and practical measures that can advance prospects for the peaceful development of all peoples'.[35] Further, the Universal House of Justice indicates that in these conferences and activities can be discerned 'the gathering momentum of an emerging unity of thought in world undertakings, the realization of which our sacred scriptures describe as one of the lights of unity that will illumine the path to peace'.[36]

The process of building the Lesser Peace through the series of conferences and summits has been described as a mosaic, with the necessary bits of the whole picture gradually being put together. The bits are apparently random and probably not conceived by their makers to fit into any particular pattern, other than being an improvement on past 'bits'. But gradually these elements are coming together, for Bahá'ís according to the divine plan, and will eventually together make a Lesser Peace. By this theory, even when the whole picture is discernible, there may well still be bits that are not in place, gaps which will need to be filled.

The process of lengthy negotiations needed before any document derived from a particular conference can be agreed can be described as forging the Lesser Peace word by word. The process is painfully slow, long and drawn out, as those who have seen it in progress can testify, and the end product not always clear, nevertheless the determination of the negotiators to fix on a particular word or phrase that best describes the negotiated position and the care with which it is done highlights the nature of any peace negotiated in this way: a political settlement rather than the peace of the Most Great Peace.

An interesting developing of recent months has been the proposal put forward by the Commission for Global Governance that a World Conference on Global Governance be held in 1998. Already deliberations and initiatives have begun around the report of the Commission, published as *Our Global Neighbourhood*. Several non-governmental organizations (NGOs) in many countries are beginning to explore the report's proposals and there is some movement towards lobbying governments to support the idea of such a conference being sponsored by the UN.

Indicator 2: 'the Calamity'

Like the Lesser Peace itself, there is much speculation about the calamity, its nature and timing. Some Bahá'ís believe the calamity itself will 'suddenly occur' ('big bang') while others believe we are in the midst of a calamity that has been slowly overtaking humankind since the rejection of the message of Bahá'u'lláh by the kings and rulers in 1868. Indeed, a letter written on behalf of the Universal House of Justice states that 'calamities have been and are occurring and will continue to happen until mankind has been chastened sufficiently to accept the Manifestation for this day'.[37] There can be no doubt that the world has witnessed even greater tribulation since these lines were written two decades ago. That the atrocities of two World Wars, the wars in Biafra, Vietnam and Cambodia, together with the recurrent famines in sub-Saharan Africa and the periodic flooding of the Indian plains have not been yet sufficient to chasten mankind makes one wonder what more might be in store for the world.

John Hatcher, in *The Arc of Ascent*, suggests that the calamity needs to be something from which mankind can learn, not merely a collection of earthquakes or aliens invading from outer space: 'we can infer that the lessons it will impart will be unmistakably apparent: that unbridled materialism is a perverse motive for human governance, that material well-being is an insufficient criterion by which to judge human success or justice, and that a planetary system of governance in all its manifestations is not merely feasible but the only option available for human survival.'[38] Thus, 'a "natural disaster" . . . while capable of causing us to rethink our priorities, would not seem to convey the very clear message that we are responsible for our own sordid condition nor would it cause us to see in this event the logical necessity of rethinking our identity or reorganizing our governmental structures to guard against any such calamity ever recurring.'[39]

This seems to be borne out by the words of Shoghi Effendi quoted above, as 'war, famine and pesti-lence'— generally the result of human action (or inaction)—are often the disasters which most effectively 'stir the conscience of the world'.

Indicator 3: The 'reconstruction of mankind, as the result of the universal recognition of its oneness and wholeness'[40]
Is the Lesser Peace bound up with the general recognition of the oneness of humankind? Do we have to recognize this before we can get the Lesser Peace, or can the Lesser Peace be established and then we find it? The Universal House of Justice suggests that the two are intimately linked.

The primary question to be resolved is how the present world, with its entrenched pattern of conflict, can change to a world in which harmony and co-operation will prevail.

World order can be founded only on an unshakable consciousness of the oneness of mankind, a spiritual truth which all the human sciences confirm. Anthropology, physiology, psychology, recognize only one human species, albeit infinitely varied in the secondary aspects of life. Recognition of this truth requires abandonment of prejudice—prejudice of every kind—race, class, colour, creed, nation, sex, degree of material civilization, everything which enables people to consider themselves superior to others.

Acceptance of the oneness of mankind is the first fundamental prerequisite for reorganization and administration of the world as one country, the home of humankind. Universal acceptance of this spiritual principle is essential to any successful attempt to establish world peace . . .[41]

Can it be said that there is a universal 'consciousness of the oneness of mankind'? If such a consciousness is considered to be reflected in those instruments which have been agreed by a number of Sates, e.g. the Charter of the United Nations and the Universal Declaration of Human Rights, then to that extent it can be argued that recognition of the oneness of humanity has been formally and politically accepted. This is an improvement over the situation before 1945, where it was politically and legally determined in, for example,

Germany, that certain sections of humanity were certainly not part of a whole. Further, progress seems even greater when we consider the attitude of colonizers to the peoples they colonized, or slavers to the enslaved.

However, this has not yet led to the 'reconstruction' of humanity. Racism has not only not been overcome, but appears on the increase in certain societies. Anti-Semitism, hidden in Eastern Europe for decades, has reappeared. Women are still denied equal access to education, employment and other opportunities. Despite the recent conference on the rights of the child, child abuse is widespread and the use of child forced and slave labour apparently undiminished in eastern countries. The rights of the disabled and mentally unwell continue to go unrecognized in many States, while in China, for example, the mentally ill and disabled are to be sterilized (perhaps a thinly veiled attempt to punish political—and religious—dissidents?). Clearly, simply making a declaration to the effect that 'humanity is one' does not necesssarilly make it a living reality.

Indicator 4: 'the inevitable curtailment of unfettered national sovereignty'[42]

'Sovereignty—the principle that a State has supreme authority over all matters that fall within its territorial domain—is the cornerstone of the modern interstate system'[43] and has been since the Treaty of Westphalia in 1648. The principle of the sovereignty of States is based on concepts of territoriality, impermeability and political independence, together with the principle of the legal equality of States. The principle of sovereignty is upheld by the UN Charter through non-intervention in the domestic affairs of other countries.

The stability of the sovereign State system has always been somewhat in doubt, as the edges of what does and does not constitute a State's internal affairs are blurred. Throughout the Cold War, the mutual mistrust of the so-called 'super powers' was fuelled, to some extent, by ideological differences, one side calling for a worldwide revolution in order to establish a commonwealth of States ruled by 'dictatorships of the proletariat', while the other maintained political and economic colonies and lived off the fruits of imperialism. As the international political scene has moved away from a bi-polar system, it has become more difficult 'to separate actions that solely affect a nation's internal affairs from those that have an impact on the internal affairs of other states, and hence to define the legitimate boundaries of sovereign states'.[44] It has become obvious that certain problems are not limited to national boundaries—for instance pollution, terrorism, criminality and drug trafficking—increasingly governments are willing to work together to tackle these issues and the erosion of sovereignty has led to an increased level of multilateral actions. The establishment of the information highway and the increased level of international money dealing and multinational transactions has made national boundaries even more permeable.

As a result, the Commission for Global Governance has concluded that 'Increasingly, countries are having to accept that in certain fields sovereignty has to be exercised collectively'.[45] Thus the curtailment of unfettered sovereignty has become 'inevitable'. Nevertheless politicians in States such as the United Kingdom continue to use the rhetoric of sovereignty, particularly to their domestic constituents, in situations where decisions taken by outside bodies (e.g. the European Parliament) are deemed to be against the national interest—generally when those decisions are critical of, in opposition to, or override national policies and legislation. Where such international (or European) legislation is in harmony with national legislation, there are only rare appeals to the principle of sovereignty.

Thus there is, on the one hand, an inexorable move towards a different definition of sovereignty that takes into account the need for States to work together in certain areas and, on the other, a need for States to feel that such a move is within their control and not imposed from outside. States' fear of global government is based just on this concern—a loss of power over their own internal affairs and absorption by some ill-willed, abusive, self-styled global government whose sole interests are the extension and maintenance of its own power. The Bahá'í belief that any world government will come about through the political will of the nations and that they will 'willingly' give up only certain aspects of sovereignty (rather than be coerced into it) is some counter to this legitimate concern. That the aspects of sovereignty called for by Shoghi Effendi so to be given up are not as yet included among those already eroded—the right to make war, to some forms of taxation and to keep unlimited armaments—is itself a measure of how much further the world needs to move in order for the Lesser Peace to be achieved.

Indicator 5: 'a political unity arrived at by decision of the governments of the various nations'[46]

The 1990s has seen a dramatic rise in the willingness of States to work together in areas of mutual interest and from which mutual benefit can be drawn, soft political areas such as the environment, the control of drug trafficking and terrorism. In areas which are close to the political bone of power—the hard political area—States appear much less willing to work together. There has been much discussion about the pros and, mostly, the cons of political unity and hardly any movement towards it. There have been a number of moves towards economic cooperation and even unity but no overt moves towards political unity or federation, such as is required by the Bahá'í model of government.

There are several countries that are federations of lesser political units—the United States being perhaps the most successful and stable model, and indeed Shoghi Effendi presents the United States as an example of what can be achieved in this direction.[47] However, the European Union is perhaps the closest attempt we have to achieving this aim in that it is one of its avowed goals, although some backtracking has taken place on this subject of late, even by France, its greatest proponent.

Thus while political unity of the kind often dreamed of by Bahá'ís has not yet occurred, nevertheless a kind of political unity, far short of federation, is occurring. The eagerness of newly-born States, in the 1960s particularly, to join the United Nations to legitimize their international status inevitably involved them in activities of global magnitude, widening particularly the base of the UN peace-keeping forces. At another level, the ending of the Cold War bipolar system has thrown international politics into a period of transition, the end of which is far from clear. The international community is still trying to come to terms with the new situation and even among international relations theorists there is no consensus on what the post-Cold War future may bring. However, whereas in the Cold War era the idea that States might *willingly* pool their political aspirations was virtually unthinkable, it is today a distinct possibility among several options.

The emergence of Japan, other Pacific rim countries, Brazil and India as major international economic players has further altered the Cold War relationships, focusing attention away from the traditional western powers and the international political system they developed and opening up new possibilities for economic and political integration and/or unity. As the old patterns are no longer the only patterns of international relationship, here again we may see developing a different set of rules and expectations from the international system that may be closer to Bahá'í expectations.

Indicator 6: evolution of 'some form of a world super-state'[48]
Whilst it is clear that no such world super-state exists today, it can be said that some of its elements are evolving.

THE INTERNATIONAL EXECUTIVE: whilst presently inadequate 'to enforce supreme and unchallengeable authority on every recalcitrant member' of the international community, a revamped UN Security Council might well fulfil this role. The Security Council is 'specifically charged with ensuring peace and security in the world'[49] and is the only organ of the UN that can take decisions that are binding on all member States, using the collective security provisions of Chapter VII of the Charter. During the Cold War the Security Council was considerably weakened in its ability to act by the use of the veto. The membership of the Security Council (permanent seats and veto powers were granted to the five 'leading' victors of World War II—the United States, the Soviet Union, the United Kingdom, France and China—with a rotating membership of other countries) is another weakness, built on post-war assumptions about the ability of non-victors to guarantee the noble provisions of the Charter. The recommendations proposed by the Commission on Global Governance address these weakness and might well give it the legitimacy and power to fulfil the role envisioned for it in the

Charter. There is certainly no other international institution on the horizon that comes anywhere near the Security Council as a possible contender for the role of the international executive. The only other alternative is to start from scratch with a wholly new institution and while there are some NGOs promoting this concept, no actual steps have been taken to create this at present.

THE WORLD PARLIAMENT: the European Parliament may be considered a model for a future world parliament , as its members are 'elected by the people in their respective countries' and it functions as a legislating body for the European member States. There is no other international equivalent. The UN General Assembly is a forum of States as States, not of representatives of the people. It is not, nor was it intended to be, a legislative body—it was always a place for deliberation. Proposed reforms of the General Assembly do not envision it as having a legislative role.

There have been suggestions and tentative moves to create a world parliament. For example, the World Constitution and Parliament Association has put forward a *Proposed Constitution for the Federation of the Earth,* which provides for a tri-cameral legislature drawn from people, governments and universities and the *We the People* movement has put forward similar ideas. While there is some popular support for these ideas among NGOs, governments have shown little interest in developing these ideas further.[50]

THE SUPREME TRIBUNAL: the World Court has existed in

its present form since 1946 and is the principal legal organ of the United Nations. The fifteen judges are elected by the UN and are drawn from different legal systems from around the world. The International Court of Justice Handbook (1986) states that 'there is today no other judicial organ in the world which has the same capacity for dealing with the problems of the international community as a whole and offers States so wide a range of opportunities for promoting the rule of law'.[51] Whilst the judgement of the Court does not have 'a binding effect even in such cases where the parties concerned did not voluntarily agree to submit their case to its consideration',[52] States do have a duty under the UN Charter to solve their disputes by peaceful means; the voluntary submission of a dispute to the Court is one of those means.

In January 1994 the Secretary General of the UN said that 'it must . . . be acknowledged that international justice has not yet—far from it—become part, if I may venture to say, of the customs of States.' He called for the 'popularization' of international justice and the extension of the use of the Court. To date, only 57 member States have accepted the compulsory jurisdiction of the Court; the UK is the only permanent member of the Security Council that has done so.

The Commission for Global Governance concluded that 'in an ideal world, acceptance of the compulsory jurisdiction of the World Court would be a prerequisite for UN membership',[53] suggesting reforms that might allay member States's fears, and give them more confidence in the Court.

The translation of the present Court into the court envisioned in the Bahá'í Writings would not be difficult, although the method of the selection of its members would need to be altered.

THE INTERNATIONAL FORCE: the Bahá'í Writings call for the establishment of a international police or peace-keeping force.[54] UN peace-keeping operations have increased dramatically in the last half decade (from 14 in the years between 1948 and 1989, to 25 in the period 1989 to the present). The lack of success in certain of its operations is due to a number of factors: the expectation that the UN will not only act as buffer between warring factions but that it will also provide humanitarian aid to civilians, putting a larger burden on the forces than had been envisioned; financial constraints; lack of confidence in the integrity and ability of the UN command; and the unwilling of the UN to intervene in domestic disputes. For the present UN peace-keeping forces to be considered as the international force envisioned by the Bahá'í writings these failings would need to be remedied, not only at the UN level, but at the State level as well.

Shoghi Effendi envisioned the Lesser Peace as having certain characteristics, described above. Of these, perhaps most progress has been made in the area of the establishment of a 'single code of international law', which is the subject of another paper of this conference. I believe these characteristics will be the fruit of the establishment of world government and the Lesser Peace, not necessarily preludes to it.

Indicator 7: Statements of the Universal House of Justice
The Universal House of Justice itself, as we have seen, often indicates the level of progress the world has made towards the Lesser Peace. For example, in 1990 the House of Justice wrote that 'we cannot forget that the dark passage of the Age of Transition has not yet been fully traversed; it is as yet long, slippery and tortuous'.[55]

In 1991 we find the Universal House of Justice stating that the response of the nations of the world to the Gulf War was a step towards the kind of collective security called for by Bahá'u'lláh as the basis of the Lesser Peace.[56]

In 1995, commenting on the effect of the World Summit for Social Development held in March in Copenhagen, the Universal House of Justice stated:

> But however little may be the immediate influence of such events on the policies of governments, however much the vast majority of the world's population may disregard or be unaware of them, their successive occurrence indicates to any Bahá'í observer a gradual movement towards the ultimate fulfilment of the will of Bahá'u'lláh that the rulers of nations meet to consult and decide on the outstanding issues confronting an increasingly global society . . .
>
> As such world events take place with increased intensity, we can see more clearly the drawing closer together of the parallel processes about which Shoghi

Effendi wrote several decades ago: the one leading to the political union of nations, the other to the ultimate union of hearts in one common faith.[57]

No doubt the letters of the Universal House of Justice will continue to help Bahá'ís make sense of the rapidly changing international political scene as its moves inexorably on towards its destiny.[58]

Conclusion

Obviously no one can say exactly when the Lesser Peace will arrive. The Universal House of Justice, in 1989, stated that 'the precise circumstances attending the establishment of the Lesser Peace are not known to us; even its exact timing is concealed in the Major Plan of God'.[59] On the other hand, the Universal House of Justice stated to the Bahá'í youth in 1983 that they would live their lives 'in a period when the forces of history are moving to a climax, when mankind will see the establishment of the Lesser Peace, and during which the Cause of God will play an increasingly prominent role in the reconstruction of human society'.[60]

That we are close to the establishment of the Lesser Peace seems clear, from the reported sayings of `Abdu'l-Bahá, confirmed by Shoghi Effendi and the Universal House of Justice. That certain features of it are slowly developing is also obvious. That we have far to go in creating all aspects of it is certain. The challenge posed by the Universal House of

Justice in 1985 still stands: will humanity choose the path of untold sorrow or of consultation? If the proposal put forward by the Commission on Global Governance for a World Conference on Global Governance is accepted, this may go a long way towards fulfilling the need for a convocation of world leaders. Indicators seem to swing both ways, but with time running out, and the statements of Shoghi Effendi so clear, it appears that unless the international community gets its collective act together, the former course will be taken.

Appendix: recent events in light of the Bahá'í Writings on world order

1) *Evidence of the unfolding world order and movement towards the Lesser Peace:*

the recent round of UN development summits and con fer ences;

the work of the Commission on Global Governance and its recommendation for a world summit;

the pulling down of the Berlin wall;

the apparent collapse of communism;

the ending of the Cold War and bipolar international political relations;

the dismantling of apartheid in South Africa;

the peace initiatives in Northern Ireland;

the apparent decline in the immediate threat of nuclear war;

the down-sizing in armaments;

the effects of the Bahá'í Holy Year (1992-3).

2) *Evidence of the 'rolling up' of the old world order:*
events in Somalia, Bosnia, Rwanda;
resurgence of communism in some previously communist
    bloc countries;
continuance and increase in racism and racial attacks;
problems with the Beijing Fourth World Conference on
    Women;
resurgence of extreme right wing views;
resurgence of fundamentalism;
the more rapid resort to violence, internationally and
    domestically, and within families and communities;
the use of violence as a recreation;
increase in political sleaze.

3) *Recent developments that can be seen either as positive
steps towards the Lesser Peace or obstacles to it:*
the development of the European Union;
efforts to create a single European currency;
development of a trade community in North America;
other such regional efforts;
recommendations of the Commission on Global Governance for global governance (rather than 'world
    government');
the reassertion of nationhood among former communist
    bloc countries.

Notes & references

1. John Galsworthy, *Swan Song* (Harmondsworth: Penguin, 1968 ed.), pp. 240-1.

2. Shoghi Effendi, *The World Order of Bahá'u'lláh: Selected Letters,* 1st pocket-sized ed. (Wilmette, Ill: Bahá'í Publishing Trust, 1991), pp. 34-5.

3. The Universal House of Justice, letter dated 31 January 1985, *Peace: A Compilation* comp. the Research Department of the Universal House of Justice (London: Bahá'í Publishing Trust, 1985), p. 45.

4. Shoghi Effendi, *The Promised Day is Come*, rev. ed. (Wilmette, Ill: Bahá'í Publishing Trust, 1980), p. 122.

5. Idem, *World Order*, p. 40.

6. Ibid.

7. Ibid.

8. Ibid.. pp. 40-1.

9. Ibid. p. 203.

10. `Abdu'l-Bahá, *The Promulgation of Universal Peace: Talks Delivered by `Abdu'l-Bahá during His Visit to the United States and Canada in 1912*, comp. Howard MacNutt, 2nd ed. (Wilmette, Ill: Bahá'í Publishing Trust, 1982), p. 167.

11. See, for example, Bahá'u'lláh, *Gleanings from the Writings of Bahá'u'lláh*, comp. and trans. Shoghi Effendi, rev. ed. (London: Bahá'í Publishing Trust, 1978), CXIX, p. 253.

12. Shoghi Effendi, *World Order*, p. 41.

13. "Abdu'l-Bahá anticipated that the Lesser Peace could be established before the end of the twentieth century.' (From a letter written on behalf of the Universal House of Justice to an individual, dated 15 April 1976, in Helen Bassett Hornby, comp., *Lights of Guidance: A Bahá'í Reference File*, 3rd rev. ed. [New Delhi: Bahá'í Publishing Trust, 1994], 427, p. 128).

'Now in this world of being, the Hand of Divine Power hath

firmly laid the foundations of this all-highest Bounty and this wondrous Gift. Gradually whatsoever is latent in the innermost of this Holy
Cycle shall appear and be made manifest, for now is but the beginning
of its growth and the dayspring of the revelation of its Signs. Ere the
close of this Century and of this Age, it shall be made clear and
manifest how wondrous was that Springtide and how heavenly was that
Gift!' (`Abdu'l-Bahá, cited in Shoghi Effendi, *Bahá'í Administration*,
5th rev. ed. [Wilmette, Ill: Bahá'í Publishing Trust, 1974] , pp. 15-16)

'Every century holds the solution of one predominating problem.
Although there may be many problems, yet one of the innumerable
problems will loom large and become the most important of all . . . in
this luminous century the greatest bestowal of the world of humanity
is Universal Peace, which must be founded, so that the realm of
creation may obtain composure, the East and the West, which include
in their arms the five continents of the globe, may embrace each other,
mankind may rest beneath the tent of oneness of the world of humanity, and the flag of universal peace may wave over all the regions.'
(`Abdu'l-Bahá, cited in George O. Latimer, comp., 'The Social
Teachings of the Bahai Movement', *Star of the West*, vol. VII [bound
vol. 4, Oxford: George Ronald Publisher, 1978], p. 136).

'It is true that `Abdu'l-Bahá made statements linking the establish-
ment of the unity of nations to the twentieth century. For example: 'The
fifth candle is the unity of nations -- a unity which, in this century, will
be securely established, causing all the peoples of the world to regard
themselves as citizens of one common fatherland.' And, in *The
Promised Day Is Come*, following a similar statement quoted from
Some Answered Questions, Shoghi Effendi makes this comment: 'This
is the stage which the world is now approaching, the stage of world
unity, which, as `Abdu'l-Bahá assures us, will, in this century, be
securely established.'

'There is also this statement from a letter written in 1946 to an individual believer on behalf of the beloved Guardian by his secretary: "All we know is that the Lesser and the Most Great Peace *will* come —their exact dates we do not know".' (From a letter written by the Universal House of Justice, dated 29 July 1974, *Peace*, pp. 42-3).

14. `Abdu'l-Bahá, `*Abdu'l-Bahá in Canada*, comp. National Spiritual Assembly of the Bahá'ís of Canada (Toronto: National Spiritual Assembly of the Bahá'ís of Canada, 1962), p. 35.

15. In 1934, in answer to a question, a letter written on behalf of Shoghi Effendi clarified the nature of the World Executive somewhat: 'As regards the International Executive referred to by the Guardian in his 'Goal of a New World Order' it should be noted that this statement refers by no means to the Bahá'í Commonwealth of the future, but simply to that world government which will herald the advent and lead to the final establishment of the World Order of Bahá'u'lláh. The formation of this International Executive, which corresponds to the executive head or board in present-day national governments, is but a step leading to the Bahá'í world government of the future, and hence should not be identified with either the institution of the Guardianship or that of the International House of Justice.' (From a letter written on behalf of Shoghi Effendi to an individual, dated 17 March 1934, Hornby, op. cit., 1077, p. 321).

The institution about which the most has been written is the Supreme Tribunal. This is possibly because people asked about it, through their confusion between it and the Universal House of Justice. In any case, `Abdu'l-Bahá spoke more about it than any of the other institutions of the Lesser Peace: 'A Supreme Tribunal shall be elected by the peoples and governments of every nation, where members from each country and government shall assemble in unity. All disputes shall be brought before this Court, its mission being to prevent war'. (`Abdu'l-Bahá, *Paris Talks: Addresses Given by `Abdu'l-Bahá in 1911*, 12th rev. ed. [London: Bahá'í Publishing Trust, 1995], 40:28, p. 135).

'A Supreme Tribunal shall be established by the peoples and Governments of every nation, composed of members elected from each country and Government. The members of this Great Council shall assemble in unity. All disputes of an international character shall be submitted to this Court, its work being to arrange by arbitration everything which otherwise would be a cause of war. The mission of this Tribunal would be to prevent war.' (Ibid., 48:1, p. 161).

'. . . the question of universal peace, about which Bahá'u'lláh says that the Supreme Tribunal must be established . . . the Supreme Tribunal which Bahá'u'lláh has described will fulfil this sacred task with the utmost might and power. And his plan is this: that the national assemblies of each country and nation—that is to say parliaments—should elect two or three persons who are the choicest men of that nation, and are well informed concerning international laws and the relations between governments and aware of the essential needs of the world of humanity in this day. The number of these representatives should be in proportion to the number of inhabitants of that country. The elections of these souls who are chosen by the National Assembly, that is, the parliament, must be confirmed by the upper house, the congress and the cabinet and also by the president or monarch so these persons may be the elected ones of all the nation and the government. From among these people the members of the Supreme Tribunal will be elected, and all mankind will thus have a share therein, for every one of these delegates is fully representative of his nation. When the Supreme Tribunal gives its ruling on any international question, either unanimously or by majority rule, there will no longer be any pretext for the plaintiff or ground of objection for the defendant. In case any of the governments or nations, in the execution of the irrefutable decision of the Supreme Tribunal, be negligent or dilatory, the rest of the nations will rise up against it, because all the governments and nations of the world are the supporters of this Supreme Tribunal. Consider what a firm foundation this is!' (Idem, *Selections from the Writings of `Abdu'l-Bahá*, comp. Research Department of the Universal House of Justice, trans. a committee at the Bahá'í World Centre and by Marzieh Gail, rev. ed. [Haifa: Bahá'í World Centre, 1982], 227, pp. 306-7).

In 1945 Shoghi Effendi reiterated the nature of the Supreme Tribunal, possibly refuting a suggestion that it was the same institution as the Universal House of Justice, a view still commonly held today: 'The Supreme Tribunal is an aspect of a World Superstate; the exact nature of its relationship to that State we cannot present foresee.

'Supreme Tribunal is the correct translation; it will be a contributing factor in establishing the Lesser Peace.' (From a letter written on behalf of Shoghi Effendi to an individual, dated 19 November 1945, Hornby, op. cit, 1074, p. 320).

It appears that a later stage in the development of the world commonwealth, to be established some time after the Lesser Peace, is described by Shoghi Effendi in 1936 (*World Order*, pp. 203-6) rather than merely a refinement of his earlier description. Indeed, the Research Department of the Universal House of Justice seems to bear out this proposition in its memorandum of 10 September 1990 on World Government and the Universal House of Justice: 'a second, more distant, stage in the evolution of a system of world government, i.e. the "world commonwealth", is described in "The Unfoldment of World 'Civilization" in the book *The World Order of Bahá'u'lláh*.'

16. Shoghi Effendi, *Messages to the Bahá'í World 1950-1957* (Wilmette, Ill: Bahá'í Publishing Trust, 1958), p. 74.

17. 'Bahá'u'lláh's principal mission in appearing at this time in human history is the realization of the oneness of mankind and the establishment of peace among the nations; therefore, all the forces which are focused on accomplishing these ends are influenced by His Revelation. We know, however, that peace will come in stages. First, there will come the Lesser Peace, when the unity of nations will be achieved,

then gradually the Most Great Peace—the spiritual as well as social and political unity of mankind, when the Bahá'í World Commonwealth, operating in strict accordance with the laws and ordinances of the Most Holy Book of the Bahá'í Revelation, will have been established through the efforts of Bahá'ís.

'As to the Lesser Peace, Shoghi Effendi has explained that this will initially be a political unity arrived at by the decision of the governments of various nations; it will not be established by direct action of the Bahá'í community. This does not mean, however that the Bahá'ís are standing aside and waiting for the Lesser Peace to come before they do something about the peace of mankind. Indeed, by promoting the principles of the Faith, which are indispensable to the maintenance of peace, and by fashioning the instruments of the Bahá'í Administrative Order, which we are told by the beloved Guardian is the pattern for future society, the Bahá'ís are constantly engaged in laying the groundwork for a permanent peace, the Most Great Peace being their ultimate goal.

'The Lesser Peace itself will pass through stages; at the initial stage the governments will act entirely on their own without the conscious involvement of the Faith; later on, in God's good time, the Faith will have a direct influence on it in ways indicated by Shoghi Effendi in his 'The Goal of a New World Order'. In connection with the steps that will lead to this latter stage, the Universal House of Justice will certainly determine what has to be done, in accordance with the guidance in the Writings, such as the passage you quoted from 'Tablets of Bahá'u'lláh', page 89. In the meantime, the Bahá'ís will undoubtedly continue to do all in their power to promote the establishment of peace.' (From a letter written on behalf of the Universal House of Justice, dated 31 January 1985, *Peace*, p. 45).

18. Other such passages include: 'O ye peoples of the would! Know, verily, that an unforeseen calamity followeth you, and grievous

retribution awaiteth you. Think not that which ye have committed hath been effaced in My sight.' (Bahá'u'lláh, *Gleanings*, CIV, p. 209)

'The House of Justice points out that calamities have been and are occurring and will continue to happen until mankind has been chastened sufficiently to accept the Manifestation for this day. `Abdu'l-Bahá anticipated that the Lesser Peace could be established before the end of the twentieth century. However, Bahá'ís should not be diverted from the work of the Cause by the fear of catastrophes but should try to understand why they occur. The beloved Guardian, in innumerable places, has explained the reasons for these occurrences, and since they happen from time to time as explained above we should not be concerned as to when they occur'. (From a letter written on behalf of the Universal House of Justice to an individual, dated 15 April 1976, Hornby, op. cit. 427, p. 128).

19. Bahá'u'lláh, *Gleanings*, LXI, p. 118.

20. Shoghi Effendi, *World Order*, pp. 193-4. This was written in 1936.

21. Shoghi Effendi, *Promised Day is Come*, pp. 122-3.

22. Shoghi Effendi, *Citadel of Faith: Messages to America, 1947-1957* (Wilmette, Ill: Bahá'í Publishing Trust, 1965), pp. 31-3.

23. The Universal House of Justice, *Wellspring of Guidance: Messages from the Universal House of Justice*, rev. ed. (Wilmette, Ill: Bahá'í Publishing Trust, 1976), p. 120.

24. The Universal House of Justice, Ridván Message to the Bahá'ís of the world, 1990, *A Wider Horizon: Selected Messages of the Universal House of Justice 1983-1992*, comp. Paul Lample (Riviera Beach, Fla: Palabra Publications, 1992), p. 82. At the same time, the Bahá'í Faith itself is passing through the first of a series of 'successive stages of unmitigated obscurity, of active repression and of complete emancipation, leading in turn to its being acknowledged as an independent Faith . . .' (Shoghi Effendi, *The Advent of Divine Justice*, 1st pocket-sized ed. (Wilmette, Ill: Bahá'í Publishing Trust, 1990), p. 15) which will

eventually lead it to being an influence on the progress of the period of the Lesser Peace in the first instance, and later to the merging of the institutions of the Lesser Peace with those anticipated by Bahá'u'lláh for the Most Great Peace. In May 1995 the Universal House of Justice stated that 'the Faith has emerged from obscurity . . .' (letter to National Spiritual Assemblies, 5 May 1995), so we can expect now to enter the phase of active repression. That this stage in the development of the Faith coincides in time so closely with the anticipated calamity cannot be a mere coincidence.

See also note 58 for the most recent statement by the Universal House of Justice on the condition of the world—and of the Bahá'í community—in relation to the advent of the Lesser Peace.

25. Before we consider this question perhaps we should ask ourselves, what weight do we give the writings of Bahá'u'lláh, the writings of 'Abdu'l-Bahá, the recorded words of 'Abdu'l-Bahá and the writings of Shoghi Effendi? Can we assume, for instance, that the Guardian could see into the future and know what the institutions of the Lesser Peace look like? 'Abdu'l-Bahá? For Bahá'ís there is no question about Bahá'u'lláh's ability to do so, I assume, but in this area He does not give details, only the general outlines cited above.

I take the position that both 'Abdu'l-Bahá and Shoghi Effendi, as expounders of the word of God, were not able to see into the future but were able to elucidate the writings of Bahá'u'lláh, who could. Therefore they both extrapolated from the writings of Bahá'u'lláh that certain events were to take place and, knowing Bahá'u'lláh's mind, so to speak, were able to demonstrate how His predictions would take place, thus having the effect of prophesying themselves. In the case of the Lesser Peace, this 'prophecy' was the natural spinning out of Bahá'u'lláh's statements joined to world events and an understanding of those events based on the theory of history propounded by Bahá'u'lláh. That is, that God intervenes in history to the extent of sending His prophets, and that recent world events are the product of the renewal of God's message in this day. Thus Bahá'ís see the political history of the world community as its attempt to develop ever more encompassing forms of government—beginning with the social unit of the family, through clan banding, tribal groupings, the development of nations and its corollary of the State, through attempts at State grouping in economic or quasi-political units. The final stage, according to the Bahá'í writings, is a global grouping under a world government. Bahá'ís believe this is an inevitable step in the social evolution of the planet. They view the political history of the world over the past century as a series of ever more successful attempts to establish this system. Therefore, to be brief and simplistic, the nineteenth century alliance system broke down and produced the First World War. The resolution of this war saw early attempts to regulate international political affairs through the League of Nations. This blighted attempt itself broke down and was unequal to the task of preventing a second world war. The outcome of that war saw a more vigorous attempt to establish some sort of universal political watchdog, in the form of the United Nations, an organization with more 'teeth' than the League and to which more States could subscribe. The struggle of the world community of States to come to terms with the global nature of its concerns has not been yet wholly met by the United Nations, and it may be that this attempt, too, will fail, although Bahá'ís are strong supporters of its peace-keeping and development activities. This view of international political history by Bahá'ís gives them reason to believe that the establishment of the prophesied world government is inevitable.

26. Bahá'u'lláh, *Gleanings*, CXVII, p. 249.

27. `Abdu'l-Bahá, *The Secret of Divine Civilization*, trans. Marzieh Gail, 1st pocket size ed. (Wilmette, Ill: Bahá'í Publishing Trust, 1994), p. 64.

28. Ibid. pp. 64-5.

29. Ibid. p. 65.

30. Bahá'u'lláh, *Gleanings*, CXVII, p. 248.

31. Ibid.

32. The Universal House of Justice, *The Promise of World Peace*, rev. ed. (London: Bahá'í Publishing Trust, 1992), p. 20.

33. Shoghi Effendi, *Citadel of Faith*, p. 33.

34. It is interesting to reflect on why this might be so. Only 51 States attended the conference and became founding members of the UN, representing 70 per cent of the world's people (*Our Global Neighborhood: The Report of the Commission on Global Governance* [New York: Oxford University Press, 1995], p. 8). Much of the world, including almost all of sub-Saharan Africa, was still under colonial rule, so that first gathering of the UN members was hardly representative of the world's peoples. On the other hand, the criterion for calling the convocation is only the involvement of 'a certain number of its [the world's] distinguished and high-minded sovereigns' (`Abdu'l-Bahá, *Secret of Divine Civilization*, p. 64) so this criterion could certainly be considered to have been fulfilled by the meeting establishing the UN. However, these 'sovereigns' were to be 'the shining exemplars of devotion and determination' (ibid.). Can it be said that they were? In light of the current rumpus about political sleaze, how much do the personal lives of these leaders affect this condition? This is perhaps the basis for a research paper.

Another condition is that the leaders 'shall, for the good and happiness of all mankind, arise, with firm resolve and clear vision, to establish the Cause of Universal Peace' (ibid). Was the UN summit undertaken for the good and happiness of all mankind? The Preamble of the UN Charter states that the peoples of the world resolved 'to practise tolerance and live together in peace with one another as good neighbours', hence the Charter that formulated the methods by which this was to be achieved. And was the Charter to establish the Cause of

Universal Peace? Certainly the intention was to make war difficult, if not impossible.

However, it must be said that having set out this noble vision of intent, the framers of the Charter did not go on actually to establish the Cause of Peace by creating any sort of power within the UN that could guarantee that peace, that is, no executive force with real teeth was created.

As we have seen, ʿAbduʾl-Bahá stated that the Covenant produced by the summit had to contain certain provisions.

The Charter of the UN certainly contains elements of these provisions. However, the limitation of arms is not adequately dealt with in the UN Charter and on this ground alone the summit to establish the UN fails as the called-for convocation. Further, the basis for action against aggressors to be determined by the convocation is collective security. Whilst the intention of the UN charter was to provide for collective action, for nearly the whole of the Cold War era, only so recently ended, the use of the veto in the Security Council effectively prevented this.

35. The Universal House of Justice, cited in introduction to Baháʾí International Community, *The Prosperity of Humankind* (London: Baháʾí Publishing Trust, 1995), pp. iii-iv.

36. Ibid., p. iv.

37. From a letter written on behalf of the Universal House of Justice to an individual, dated 15 April 1976, Hornby, op. cit. 427, p. 128

38. John S. Hatcher, *The Arc of Ascent: The Purpose of Physical Reality II* (Oxford: George Ronald Publisher, 1994), p. 248.

39. Ibid. p. 249.

40. Shoghi Effendi, *Promised Day is Come*, p. 122.

41. The Universal House of Justice, *Promise of World Peace*, p. 16.

42. Shoghi Effendi, *World Order*, p. 40.

43. *Our Global Neighbourhood*, p. 68.

44. Ibid. p. 70.

45. Ibid.

46. The Universal House of Justice, letter dated 31 January 1985, *Peace*, p. 45.

47. Shoghi Effendi, *World Order*, pp. 45-6.

48. Ibid., p. 40.

49. *Our Global Neighbourhood*, p. 234.

50. Bahá'ís should note that at this stage of the development of the Bahá'í Commonwealth the Universal House of Justice is not to be considered as the world executive—see letter written on behalf of Shoghi Effendi, dated 17 March 1934. By extension, then, the Universal House of Justice should not be considered as the world parliament. In any case, the nature of its election and its membership differ markedly from that intended for the world parliament.

51. International Court of Justice Handbook (1986), p. 77.

52. Shoghi Effendi, *World Order*, p. 40.

53. *Our Global Neighbourhood*, p. 313.

54. Contrary to popular Bahá'í belief, the Bahá'í Faith does not call for complete disarmament or the abandonment of national security measures, merely the limitation of arms to a level necessary to keep the peace domestically. Exactly what this means will, no doubt, be the subject of discussion and negotiation between the world authority and its constituent federated States.

55. '. . . world society finds itself in a critical phase of its transition to the character envisioned for it by the Lord of the Age. The winds of God rage on, upsetting old systems, adding impetus to the deep yearning for a new order in human affairs . . . The rapidity of the changes being wrought stirs up the expectations which inspire our dreams in the closing decade of the twentieth century. The situation is equally a bright portent and a weighty challenge.

It is portentous of the profound change in the structure of present-day society which attainment to the Lesser Peace implies. Hopeful as are the signs, we cannot forget that the dark passage of the Age of Transition has not yet been fully traversed; it is as yet long, slippery and tortuous. For godlessness is rife, materialism rampant. Nationalism and racism still work their treachery in men's hearts, and humanity remains blind to the spiritual foundations of the solution to its economic woes. (The Universal House of Justice, Ridván Message to the Bahá'ís of the world, 1990, *A Wider Horizon*, pp. 78-9).

56. 'The forces which united the remedial reactions of so many nations to the sudden crisis in this region demonstrated beyond any doubt the necessity of the principle of collective security prescribed by Bahá'u'lláh more than a century ago as a means of resolving conflict. White the international arrangements envisioned by Him for the full application of this principle is far from having been adopted by the rulers of mankind, a long step towards the behaviour outlined for the nations by the Lord of the Age has thus been taken.' (Idem, Ridván Message to the Bahá'ís of the world, 1991, ibid., p. 85).

57. Idem, Ridván Message to the Bahá'ís of the world, 1995, *The American Bahá'í*, vol. 26, no. 4 (17 May 1995), p. 3.

58. In its 1996 Ridván message to the Bahá'ís of the world, the Universal House of Justice locates the present day Bahá'í community—and the wider world—'amid the turbulence of a period of accelerating transition. The twin processes prompted by the impact of Bahá'u'lláh's Revelation are fast at work, gathering a momentum that will, in the words of Shoghi Effendi, "bring to a climax the forces that are transforming the face of our planet." One is an integration process; the other is disruptive. Out of the "universal fermentation" created by these processes, peace will emerge in stages, through which the unifying effects of a growing consciousness of world citizenship will become manifest.

'Towards that end, recent world developments have, paradoxically, been both shocking and reassuring. On one hand, the disarray of human affairs produces a daily diet of horrors that benumb the senses; on the other, world leaders are often taking collective actions that, to a Bahá'í observer, signify a tendency towards a common approach by nations to solving world problems. Consider, for instance, the unusual frequency of the global occasions on which these leaders have gathered since the Holy Year four years ago, such as the one in observance of the Fiftieth anniversary of the United Nations, at which the attending heads of state and heads of governments asserted their commitment to world peace. Noteworthy, too, are the promptitude and spontaneity with which these government leaders have been acting together in responding to a variety of crises in different parts of the world. Such trends coincide with the increasing cries from enlightened circles for attention to be given to the feasibility of achieving some form of global governance. Might we not see in these swiftly developing occurrences the workings of the Hand of Providence, indeed the very harbinger of the monumental occasion forecast in our Writings?

'Even though the establishment of the Lesser Peace is not dependent on any Bahá'í plan or action, and although it will not represent the ultimate goal humanity is destined to reach the Golden Age, our community has a responsibility to lend spiritual impetus to the processes towards that peace. The need at this exact time is to so intensify our efforts in building the Bahá'í System that we will attract the confirmations of Bahá'u'lláh and thus invoke a spiritual atmosphere that will accrue to the quickening of these processes. . . .

'*However short the path to peace*, it will be tortuous; however promising the anticipated events that will set its course, it must mature through a long period of evolution, with its attendant tests, setbacks and conflicts, towards the moment when it will have emerged, under the direct influences of God's Faith, as the Most Great Peace. In the meantime, people everywhere will often face despair and bewilderment

149

before arriving at an appreciation of the transition in progress.'
(Emphasis added).

59. The Universal House of Justice, Ridván Message to the Bahá'ís of
the world, 1989, *A Wider Horizon*, p. 62.

60. From a letter written by the Universal House of Justice to the
European Bahá'í Youth Conference, Innsbruck, Austria, dated 4 July
1983.

BAHÁ'Í INSTITUTIONS AND HUMAN GOVERNANCE

Christopher Sprung

THE VIEWS SET OUT HERE reflect my personal understanding about an issue of far-reaching significance: the function of Bahá'í administration, or rather, of human governance based on Bahá'í thought, in relation to the state of the future world commonwealth. It is not my intention to present a universally acceptable viewpoint, but to stimulate thought and discussion.

We are only at the beginning of a scholarly approach to understanding the system generated by Bahá'u'lláh. Around forty years ago, Dr Udo Schaefer wrote the first doctoral thesis on Bahá'í administration. Only recently have we begun to develop and accept the social (therefore political) dimension of the Bahá'í Faith. We are no longer a nice, harmless movement, of no danger to anyone. At the end of the twentieth century, we have emerged from obscurity, and pose challenges and threats to all kinds of established orthodoxy.

We therefore must find a way to reconcile our unconscious, private wish to let the Bahá'í Faith remain at that nice, personal, joyous point where we found it a while ago, with the inevitable and urgent need to present it to the lost world, to desperate people, to scholars, in a way that enables them to at least grasp the unique character and the profound implications of Bahá'u'lláh's appearance.

In a time of the loss of ethics and fall of religions, a time when racialism and communism have virtually perished as political ideologies, leaving only nationalism remaining of the 'three false Gods',[1] such an attempt is rather difficult, and can easily lead to any number of misunderstandings. But still we must make this attempt. Let us begin with the first danger: to compare the world order of Bahá'u'lláh with other political or religious systems. We are told that a parallel is impossible:

> The Bahá'í Commonwealth of the future, of which this vast Administrative Order is the sole framework, is, both in theory and practice, not only unique in the entire history of political institutions, but can find no parallel in the annals of any of the world's recognized religious systems. No form of democratic government; no system of autocracy or of dictatorship, whether monarchical or republican; no intermediary scheme of a purely aristocratic order; nor even any of the recognized types of theocracy, whether it be the Hebrew Commonwealth, or the various Christian ecclesiastical organizations, or the Imamate or the Caliphate in Islám—none of these can be identified or be said to conform with the Administrative Order which the master-hand of its perfect Architect has fashioned.[2]

However, if we wish to respond to even sympathetic commentators outside the Bahá'í community, let alone those who would oppose us, we must guard against the temptation to call the Bahá'í Commonwealth of the future 'indescribable'. We cannot invent a new language to escape from the misuse of the old, and we should not try to do so. We must speak the language of those minds which have sincerely and profoundly contemplated the role of religion in society and the relation between religion and State. In this sense, then, I will use terms which many Bahá'ís may believe have no place in Bahá'í thought.

When contemplating the Bahá'í Faith's understanding and vision of human governance, particularly as lawyers, we should say a word on the nature of a future State constitution. In the future Bahá'í Commonwealth, will we have separation of religion and State? Or will there be a kind of re-union, a blending, a marriage of both? What about the rights of minorities, the protection of believers of other faiths? What are the governing institutions of such a State?

These questions—and more—must be addressed by future Bahá'í theology and legal studies. In fact, theology and legal studies are very close in our religion. We can however, even today, attempt early answers, which can serve as points for discussion, if not solid conclusions. Such thoughts still cannot be considered a scholarly hypothesis, as the foundation of our theology is still too weak.

To facilitate our approach to the Bahá'í concept of

governance, we may highlight two terms of interest —'theocracy' and 'democracy'—for a deeper, though still too brief, study.

In relation to the origin and source, the Bahá'í Faith, as well as its administration, is *divinely given*, whereas in other religions, only the revelation itself is of divine origin, while the system is *man-made*, generally speaking. A statement on behalf of Shoghi Effendi differentiates between those systems, which 'are in a sense theocracies', 'such as the Catholic Church and the Caliphate, which are not divinely given as systems, but man-made [although] partly derived from the teachings of Christ and Muhammad', and 'The Bahá'í theocracy . . . both divinely ordained as a system and, of course, based on the teachings of the Prophet Himself.'[3]

Is it therefore justified, and is it wise and preferable, to put the term 'theocracy' in the forefront of our discussions, or even to give preference to it? There is no easy answer to this question. I personally suggest we use this term with caution. We must bear in mind that 'theocracy' may not only be understood as referring to the divine origin of the Faith and its system, but can also be used in the sense of 'the rule of—or by—God'. If this would place our Faith into an uncomfortable, undesirable situation in the public eye, simply because 'rule by God' is an unpopular term in today's society, I still would not hesitate to use it. We have a number of unpopular terms in the Bahá'í Faith. My hesitation is rather supported by a solid ambiguity linked to the question: is it completely correct to suggest that the Bahá'í system means and implies 'rule by God'?

Let us first read Shoghi Effendi's illuminating vision of the unfoldment of the world order of Bahá'u'lláh, in a passage referring to the 'repercussions' of the Ten Year Crusade, which will

> contribute effectually to the acceleration of yet another process of tremendous significance which will carry the steadily evolving Faith of Bahá'u'lláh through its present stages of obscurity, of repression, of emancipation and of recognition—stages one or another of which Bahá'í national communities in various parts of the world now find themselves—to the stage of establishment, the stage at which the Faith of Bahá'u'lláh will be recognized by the civil authorities as the State Religion, similar to that which Christianity entered in the years following the death of the Emperor Constantine, a stage which must later be followed by the emergence of the Bahá'í State itself, functioning, in all religious and civil matters, in strict accordance with the laws and ordinances of the Kitáb-i-Aqdas, the Most Holy, the Mother Book of the Bahá'í Revelation, a stage which, in the fullness of time, will culminate in the establishment of the World Bahá'í Commonwealth, functioning in the plenitude of its powers, and which will signalize the long-awaited advent of the Christ- promised Kingdom of God on earth

—the Kingdom of Bahá'u'lláh—mirroring however faintly upon this humble handful of dust the glories of the Abhá Kingdom.[4]

Speaking of 'State Religion' and 'Bahá'í State', this thrilling and far-reaching statement made by the Guardian of course inclines us to suppose a more theocratic nature of the Bahá'í system. If we but see all aspects of the Bahá'í system however, a 'theocratic' focus of future civilization seems a one-sided approach. I dare to suggest that the emphasis of the future Bahá'í world commonwealth lays more on the *rule of the people*—purified by the Holy Spirit acting through the channels of the new world order—rather than on the *rule of order* mystified by 'holy people' claiming to rule on behalf of God. The whole focus of the appearance of Bahá'u'lláh is to transform the individual. Only such transformation will make the institutions of future Bahá'í society distinct from the old, will enable society to frame the channels for the spirit. Thus, it seems to me that the emphasis indeed is on the people rather than on the institutions.

Moreover, the term 'theocracy' was created in the period of enlightenment as a term of dispute, as an antithesis of democracy, to highlight the flaws of the church, the misuse of power by religion. The aim of the Bahá'í Faith, however, condensed in the context of the general theme of this paper, is to overcome this historically rooted understanding of religion. This aim could be described as two-fold: to ensure the potential of people to govern global affairs; and to avoid the emergence of an autocratic, over-centralized or imperialistic world super-state. I personally believe we would be well-advised to use the term theocracy in a responsible, more reluctant manner.

Now concerning 'democracy'. I believe I do not need to go into much detail here concerning that term when describing some aspects of the Bahá'í world order. Suffice to mention that we should be careful and responsible in using this term in Bahá'í context. This may sound strange in the first instance. A thorough study, however, will show that democracy, in its modern sense, provides only a few features which would be of interest to Bahá'í conceptual thinking. If it were to describe the process of electing those 'in power', it is fine, but only to a certain degree, as we know. If, however, it were to indicate that Bahá'ís stand for other major results of enlightenment and modern democracy, such as separation of church and State, the status of opposition factions, the vast power of individuals serving as chairmen or presidents or ministers of State, or the virtually unlimited regard to freedom of the individual—then we would be getting into trouble indeed.

Modern democracy is commonly described as being rule by parties or individual leaders—no longer as the rule of the people. As Bahá'í lawyers, we will find it rather easy to share with our fellow citizens our concerns about this deplorable development and to provide deeper insight on the process of decision making which is being developed in the Bahá'í world community on local, national and international levels.

In the course of discussions in Germany between a small number of Bahá'ís and a scholar of State philosophy, a proposal was developed to introduce a completely new term so as to indicate from the outset the unique character of the Bahá'í system. It was proposed to use the term *Bahá'í theonomy* (from Greek, *theos* = God; *nomos* = law). While this is certainly not a new term in scholarly circles, it could be very interesting to study in more depth the implication of this term, *theonomy: a system 'based on divine law'*. In Bahá'í sense, theonomy stands for the completely new, distinct, unique system brought by God through Bahá'u'lláh, a system which is described as the 'reconciliation' of two aspects of the one and same truth:

the Faith of Bahá'u'lláh [is] an ever-growing organism destined to become something new and greater than any of the revealed religions of the past. . . . the Faith of Bahá'u'lláh . . . will gradually produce the institutions of an ordered society, fulfilling not merely the function of the churches of the past but also the function of the civil state. By this manifestation of the Divine Will in a higher degree than in former ages, humanity will emerge from that immature civilization in which church and state are separate and competitive institutions, and partake of a true civilization in which spiritual and social principles are at last reconciled as two aspects of one and the same Truth.'[5]

Based on these, and perhaps other highly illuminating and fascinating passages from the Bahá'í Writings, I would be glad if this paper would promote further discussion of this very subject, and particularly use of the term 'Bahá'í theonomy '.

We are now, as you will realize, at a sensitive juncture in our discussions. It is a commonly accepted truth of modern thought that secularization is one of the most significant results of enlightenment and modern progress. But here we have a statement from Shoghi Effendi to the effect that separation of church and State is indicative of an immature stage of human civilization.

It is obvious that such a statement will immediately raise grave objections from the vast majority of thinkers outside the Bahá'í community. Historical processes led in painful steps to secularization. Besides a few rather noisy and powerful politicians who manipulate the religion of Islám for their own interests, virtually no one can be found to suggest that the solution of mankind's global problems could be seen in the marriage of religion and State.

However, as Bahá'ís we cannot but admit, and unhesitatingly advocate, that the future world society will be led by a supreme institution which is divinely guided and protected; that there will be no artificial 'Berlin wall' between religion

and politics, inasmuch as the Faith teaches principles concerned with the art of governance, social responsibility and
the unfoldment of civilization. Thus, the Bahá'í Faith contrib-
utes to, and aims for the shaping of society (which, after all,
is the meaning of the Greek word *politics*). 'Berlin', so to
speak, is re-united.

There follow some brief remarks on these two aspects:

The supreme institution

Naturally, all we say at this time on the future role of the
Universal House of Justice in a Bahá'í world commonwealth
which goes beyond the text is mere speculation. The text
however is thrilling enough.

In the words of `Abdu'l-Bahá, the Universal House of
Justice is the 'consummate blending of church and state'.[6]
While quotations from `Abdu'l-Bahá's public addresses do not
enjoy the kind of authority assigned to His Writings, yet this
statement is surely a strong indication of the direction in
which `Abdu'l-Bahá wished to lead us in our understanding
of the House of Justice.

Moreover, the Universal House of Justice shall occupy
a unique rank unparalleled in State and religious philosophy
and theology: 'This House of Justice enacteth the laws and the
government enforceth them. The legislative body must
reinforce the executive, the executive must aid and assist the
legislative body so that through the close union and harmony
of these two forces, the foundation of fairness and justice may

become firm and strong, that all the regions of the world may become even as Paradise itself.'[7] '. . . And as the Bahá'í Faith permeates the masses of the peoples of East and West, and its truth is embraced by the majority of the peoples of a number of Sovereign States of the world, will the Universal House of Justice attain the plenitude of its power, and exercise as the supreme organ of the Bahá'í Commonwealth all the rights, the duties and responsibilities incumbent upon the world's future superstate.'[8]

It is important for any Bahá'í jurist to be very precise in defining the elements of the future Bahá'í commonwealth. Some may already at this time be derived from the text, such as the following:

We envisage no mere union of States, neither do we advocate one world super state only, with national States having been abolished, rather, we anticipate a federalistic union with a world legislation, a world executive and a world judiciary.

We envisage this system of States operating under the principle of subsidiarity: i.e. local affairs will be addressed locally, regional affairs regionally, global matters at the global level.

The rights of minorities and the protection of the rights of the individual will be safeguarded, as a matter of principle of the Bahá'í religion.

The focus and attention of those in power will be directed towards the individual, and the individual shares responsibility with all other individuals for the world at large. This is the true meaning of unity (not uniformity), and is the operating and underlying principle of governance.

Consultation will be an established procedure of decision-making in all institutions of society, as well as in family and individual life. Consultation, in the context of this present discussion, could be seen as having two main aims: as a means of ensuring against abuse of power by the individual, and as a rational tool to define within a group the goals of the group, as well as their realization.

Religion will play the key role in establishing the set of values of society. All religions will be reconciled. A world civilization will emerge.

It is perhaps the greatest challenge for Bahá'í lawyers to draft the code of constitutional law which will be needed to serve as the basic law of the Bahá'í world commonwealth. It is my personal hope that the European Bahá'í Lawyers Association make a valuable contribution to this enterprise.

A word on politics

We know that we should 'shun politics like the plague'[9] and not be involved in partisan politics. A careful study of the text, allied with contemplation of the meaning of the word 'politics' seems to indicate three points:

1) that the principle of non-involvement in politics is a temporary measure to protect the young blossoming flower of the community of believers:

. . . Shoghi Effendi believes that for the present the Movement, whether in the East or the West, should be dissociated entirely from politics. . . . Eventually, however, as you have rightly conceived it, the Movement will, as soon as it is fully developed and recognized, embrace both religious and political issues. In fact Bahá'u'lláh clearly states that affairs of state as well as religious questions are to be referred to the House of Justice into which the Assemblies of the Bahá'ís will eventually evolve.[10]

2) That the Bahá'í Faith offers a new art of governance and social responsibility in the best sense of 'politics'. In fact, Shoghi Effendi attaches political aspects to the future Bahá'í order: 'The Bahá'í Commonwealth of the future, of which this vast Administrate Order is the sole framework, is, both in theory and practice . . . unique in the entire history of political institutions . . .'.[11]

3) That Bahá'ís will eventually assume positions of social and political responsibility: 'The Bahá'ís will be called upon to assume the reins of government when they will come to constitute the majority of the population in a given country, and even then their participation in political affairs is bound to be limited in scope unless they obtain a similar majority in some other countries as well.'[12]

I suggest that Bahá'í lawyers everywhere assume a leading role in educating the Bahá'í community in this direction. There is still much misunderstanding and misinformation on this subject in the community. If this remains unchanged, our community will not be taken seriously. I hope that the points raised in this paper may encourage further reflection and discussion.

Notes & references

1. Shoghi Effendi, *The Promised Day is Come*, rev. ed. (Wilmette: Bahá'í Publishing Trust, 1980), p. 113.

2. Idem, *The World Order of Bahá'u'lláh: Selected Letters,* 1st pocket-sized ed. (Wilmette, Ill: Bahá'í Publishing Trust, 1991), p. 152.

3. Written on behalf of Shoghi Effendi, *Directives from the Guardian*, comp. Gertrude Garrida (New Delhi: Bahá'í Publishing Trust, 1973), pp. 78-9.

4. Shoghi Effendi, *Messages to the Bahá'í World 1950-1957* (Wilmette, Ill: Bahá'í Publishing Trust, 1958), p. 155.

5. National Spiritual Assembly of the Bahá'ís of the United States and Canada, 'Concerning Membership in Non-Bahá'í Religious Organizations', *The Bahá'í World: A Biennial International Record*, vol. VI, 1934-1936 (Wilmette, Ill: Bahá'í Publishing Trust, 1937), p. 199. This statement was approved by Shoghi Effendi in letters to the National Spiritual Assembly of the Bahá'ís of the United States and Canada, dated 29 November 1935 and 11 December 1935.

6. `Abdu'l-Bahá, *The Promulgation of Universal Peace: Talks Delivered by `Abdu'l-Bahá during His Visit to the United States and Canada in 1912*, comp. Howard MacNutt, 2nd ed. (Wilmette, Ill: Bahá'í Publishing Trust, 1982), p. 455.

7. Idem, *Will and Testament of `Abdu'l-Bahá* (Wilmette, Ill: Bahá'í Publishing Trust, 1991 ed.), pp. 14-15.

8. Shoghi Effendi, *World Order*, p. 7.

9. Idem, *Directives*, p. 57.

10. From a letter written on behalf of Shoghi Effendi to an individual, dated 30 November 1930.

11. Shoghi Effendi, *World Order*, p. 152.

12. Idem, letter to an individual, dated 19 November 1939.

SERVICE TO HUMANKIND THROUGH THE LEGAL PROFESSION
Becoming a champion of justice in a corrupt and mediocre environment

Colleen E. Dawes

IN A WORLD where so many people live in fear, where children carry guns and adults carry coffins, where one of the most watched programmes on television is a live murder trial, where the universal language is graft, bribery and payoffs, it may seem that chaos and disorder reign supreme. But we know that this is not the direction in which the world is slowly moving. The Chinese have a suggestive proverb: 'There is nothing more difficult to predict than the future.' While we cannot know the future in a precise way, we do know that the consequences of present activities will have repercussions for the future. And even though, as Bahá'ís, we do not have a monopoly on a viewpoint for the future of this planet, we do have a model to offer, and, unlike all other futurists, we are in the unique position of knowing that this model will work. The practical details for implementing such a model, however, are not within our province.

Concepts such as law and order and justice are just that in today's world. We know that we live in a world where the fabric of our society is a tattered and thin rag. Too often, lawyers ignore the question of how to make the legal system effective and responsive to the existing social conditions. The world's problems are many and the internal conditions of many countries so varied that we live in a world of extremes. You may have read the recent UNICEF report that announced that five thousand children in Rwanda can be described as serial killers. And what of Bosnia?

On the international level, the policies of many governments, though less self destructive than in the 1980s, are still clearly aligned with the idea of self-help as opposed to interdependence. To understand the future—and to understand the role that lawyers can play in this future—we need to analyse the past and present; and we must know intimately the Bahá'í model for the future.

One area of hope which has grown recently—though spasmodically—is the promotion of decency in the world. An important aspect of this is the notion that poverty and mass misery are not only matters of domestic concern, but affect the quality of international life as a whole, in the present as well as in the future. Many examples attest to a global sense of the whole being affected by activities that happen in one part of the world, the acceptance of the notion that if one of us is harmed or hurt, we are all harmed or hurt, the notion of mutual interdependence. Examples of a few events that have been observed recently highlight this view. For instance, the call for help in Rwanda after the mass genocide. Help was slow in coming at first, but with the blanket media coverage showing the world what was happening in such graphic detail, many ordinary citizens could no longer keep quiet. They demanded that their leaders do something to help, or they set up charities to do what their political leaders were failing to do: collect money to buy water, or to buy medical aid. The nations' leaders could no longer ignore the plight of the Rwandans. Their constituents had forced them to act.

The world came to the rescue of the people of Kobe, and of Oklahoma City. Yet the Russians would not accept help when an earthquake devastated a city in the Sakhalin Islands. And in Kobe where there was so much damage, suffering and loss of life, the actions of many changed the hearts of all who witnessed this outpouring of assistance.

This notion of decency reflects the viewpoint that we are all one species, with one common heritage, that 'the earth is but one country and mankind its citizens'.[1] We need to grasp this rising tide of interest in the welfare of our fellows, or we risk far more devastating consequences for this planet. Yet, the world is less concerned with the moral threat posed by such disparate areas of privilege and misery, where druglords are rich and powerful leaders of mainstream western cities. We appear more concerned about the possibility of the world's nuclear arsenal getting into the hands of terrorists, of leaders reverting to less democratic forms of government. The notion of self-help still rules over interdependence.

But there are other signs of change, of a more positive

move towards a better world. Law reform is not a new concept, but there are examples which offer proof of change. In countries which follow the common law system, efforts to modernize and simplify the laws have been shown to exist since the late sixteenth century. Even in more recent times, this law reform has generally been defined within a narrow context: to get rid of antiquated laws, to make the laws more readable for the average person. An amusing case in point is how one lawyer tells another 'I will give you an orange':

> Know all men by these presents that I hereby give, grant, bargain, sell, release, convey, transfer, and quitclaim of all my right, title, interest, benefit and use whatever in, of, and concerning this chattel, otherwise known as an orange etc. etc.

Much has been said by others about how lawyers alienate the rest of the world, set themselves apart from society. But lawyers are not alone in this. The specialist language of computer professionals is another good example. As the occupational problems are just one more proof that the legal system is in trouble, no further comment will be made here. But I am sure that everyone has a few good lawyer jokes up their sleeves.

The establishment of permanent law reform bodies in many countries clearly recognizes that the task of adapting the law to fast-changing social and economic needs could not be left entirely up to the courts or to parliament. Courts do not seek to resolve social problems. Their functions are more passive, adjudicating only on those issues presented by the litigants. And the present structure of the court system creates its own defects. Who judges the judges? In a recent case which made the international news, a circuit court judge in the United States was deciding on a matter before him which dealt with a man who, upon returning home and finding his wife in bed with another man, obtained a gun and shot her in the head, fatally wounding her. The judge's comment, when stating that a prison sentence was not justified? 'What man who has been married for four or more years could walk away from such a scene without doing some harm?' The sentence: eighteen months in a detention centre.

And we know the legal system is in ruins when we consider the O.J. Simpson trial. Who was really on trial there? The winner in this case must surely be the public, because no matter what the final verdict, we know that the legal system as it presently is has been tarnished forever—but also that some change must come out of this. Too many people have witnessed the flaws of the legal system, and, just as they didn't keep quiet about Rwanda, so they will learn to let their dissatisfaction be heard about this too. We are told that the system is the way it is because it is better that five hundred guilty people go free than one innocent person go to jail. Yet in the past thirty years, in those States of the USA which have capital punishment, we know that at least thirty innocent people have been executed. And with the rise of single parent families all over the world, there is a new victim when the parent is jailed—the children, because they do their parent's time, even though that they are not in any jail that we may recognize.

The United States is just one example of a country with a legal system that needs changing. But then again, I am unable to cite any country's legal system as a model that other countries should follow. All legal systems need to be reformed. On one hand, we have a court system in many western countries that has as its goal the fair resolution of disputes. On the other, we have a system that prejudices the poor and needy, but rewards the wealthy.

Several months ago I was asked by the Universal House of Justice to meet with lawyers in Turkey to discuss a property matter that had remained unresolved for about ten years. I knew nothing about Turkish law so my brief was to get a feel for the Turkish legal system. It did not take me long to find out just how one can beat the legal system; not that we chose to take such action, but we knew what we were up against. Money plays a crucial role in Turkey, where, as is the case with many other countries, it can be used to buy what some people call justice.

Even in those countries where law reform is more progressive (in the sense that more topical studies are being undertaken with the assistance of experts in the non-legal disciplines such as anthropologists and sociologists), and community feedback about proposals is obtained), parliaments are often reluctant to accept the recommendations made to them. The problem is often the lack of political will needed to make the necessary changes; it may not exist for a multitude of reasons, including reasons that parliament may perceive as being more pressing than legal reform.

Major technological breakthroughs further demand the law be more flexible, more able to adapt to a society constantly changing at a pace undreamt of even twenty years ago. At a world futurist meeting in 1977, the then head of Digital Computers Inc., a major computer company, stated that there would be no need for computers in the home. No need to comment on his inability to predict the future! But where does the Internet fit into the next century? If steering through the internet is the equivalent to driving down a dirt road, what will happen when the full potential of the internet is realised—what will the cyberspace super highway be like and what is the potential for degradation of individual rights and freedoms? I recently watched a television mini-series which indirectly challenged the viewer to consider the full repercussions of what some recent technological developments could do. It was set only twelve years into the future, when the technology for beaming life-sized holograms into people's homes had been achieved. This isn't as far-fetched as it may sound. Interactive television currently exists and has been tested in some parts of Canada and the United States. I don't need to be a futurist to predict that the owner of such technol-

ogies in the future could hold the world to ransom by demanding such royalties that could bring him or her such
wealth that the next step would be power over much of the
world. And we all know that power corrupts and that absolute
power corrupts absolutely.

Nor have I touched on genetic engineering and the
protection required to protect its by-products such as frozen
embryos. There has been enough written about the need to
protect children who were created to satisfy some infertile
couples' desire for children, and what of the rights of surro-
gate parents? Medical breakthroughs occur at such pace that
it is difficult to predict what will happen next year let alone
next century. The legal system has failed to ensure that the
changing social conditions have created new areas equally
protected by law. And still the scientists work on producing
clones of human organs and there are others who hope that
cryogenics will work. I, personally, have no desire for clones
of myself and am pleased that life in this world has a known
end.

The legal education system is also fraught with new
challenges. Some time during the last decade, in an attempt
to introduce a new way of looking at prejudice not only in
law schools, but in the way in which language is used in
society generally, a term was coined: 'political correctness'.
The phrase means adhering to a typically progressive orthodoxy on issues involving race, gender, sexual affinity, or
ecology. Though the term was originated by a group of

people interested in raising consciousness about parts of our vocabulary with racist and sexist overtones, it has taken on a life of its own, far beyond the expectations of its originators, such that anyone who disagrees or raises doubts about the philosophical tenets behind the meaning of what is 'politically correct' runs the risk of being thought racist, sexist or homophobic.

A well known professor of law from Harvard University, Alan Dershowitz, stated that there are three areas that are most central to political correctness: 'race and gender-specific affirmative action, rape and gay rights. And it is totally unacceptable to be in favour of Israel on any matters.'[2] So much for those of us who look to Israel as the geographical location of the centre of our Faith! Some law schools have reported that there is an enormous unwillingness to even argue for the wrong side in matters that touch upon political correctness. Yet the concerns that the political correctness phrase expresses are generally real. Past injustices need to be corrected and there needs to be a re-examination of legal thought and institutions. But is this the way to go about it, by forcing people to have the same views on issues such as gay rights? Certainly we need to set standards for behaviour but is this the way to do it?

If the premise behind political correctness is acceptance of diversity, then this is a positive step, as it is asking people to accommodate a variety of perspectives. However, the tendency is to find diversity deeply threatening, particularly when the demand for diversity is arguably a cover for a political power grab by the left. If we extrapolate this view further, we find that rather than looking at the beauty that there is in diversity, political correctness teaches us to believe that there is only one way to think, and that is the 'politically correct' way. And in a snap, gone is the very diversity that political correctness started out protecting! Ironic isn't it?

It is clear that what we have in the world is no longer working. Something new is needed. And that something new is a way at looking at a new model for society, the Bahá'í model. Bahá'u'lláh compared the world to the human body, and it is to this model of a future society to which we must turn. By looking at the world as equivalent to the human body, we start to realise that there must be more implications for all our actions or omissions even if we don't see it ourselves, or don't see it immediately. We know that we can abuse our body for many years, but it will eventually catch up with us. That is what has happened to the world. It has all caught up with us, and we happen to be the privileged few who are now witnessing the breakdown of this world.

Earlier this year, the Universal House of Justice asked the Bahá'í International Community's Office of Public Information to prepare a statement on the concept of global prosperity in the context of the Bahá'í teachings. A study of the statement entitled *The Prosperity of Humankind* shows that it sets down the criteria which we can use to guide us in establishing this model. Though development concepts are at the heart of this statement, it has also acknowledged the fact that there has been a change in consciousness of the people to help each other and that is a significant step forward to this new model for the world. The responsibility for the destiny of the world must 'be the consciousness of the oneness of humankind'.[3] Some of the signs evidencing this consciousness or this rise of moral decency were mentioned briefly in the beginning of this paper.

One of the aspects of this model is the notion of unity in diversity. You will recall that there is indeed consciousness at the community level about the need for acceptance of humanity's diversity. One sign was the way we had been challenged to think about ensuring that our comments are 'politically correct'. Yet, as was mentioned earlier, the concept of political correctness is flawed because it requires all people to follow the same thought flows despite the fact that its premise was indeed the protection of diversity, or perhaps what may be better described as the protection of minorities. One reason for its flaws was because its proponents were motivated by political aspirations. We see that this motivation will bring its downfall. The motivation for ensuring acceptance of diversity is to ensure that all people are treated equally because we are all part of the human family.

The Bahá'í model 'calls for the creation of laws and institutions that are universal in both character and authority'.[4] It will require people to work together to formulate goals, to work towards the attainment of these goals. At the heart of this model is justice, and that is where lawyers need to take an active role. Bahá'u'lláh states that: 'Justice is "the best beloved of all things" since it permits each individual to see with his own eyes rather than through the eyes of others, to know through his own knowledge rather than through the knowledge of his neighbour or his group. It calls for fair-mindedness in one's own judgements, for equity in one's treatment of others, and is thus a constant if demanding companion in the daily occasions of life.'[5]

Much has been written on the various theories of justice that exist in the world. We can look at individually-oriented and civil justice, contrasted with collectively-oriented distributive justice; personal claims competing with group claims; economic justice versus political justice; nor can we ignore the international dimensions of justice. Other views such as that justice and fairness are synonymous are defective, perhaps because they limit themselves to social justice and ignore the role of the individual. On the other hand, we have many different views on the concept of justice, from procedural views to general concepts, with views of justice varying depending on the subjects or categories of justice. Nor have I discussed the effects of the struggle for justice. We often hear the rallying-cry of a revolution held in the name of justice, and, in the process, at least for a time, the revolution becomes manifestly unjust.

But there is a common factor linking all the various theories that try to explain justice. They deal with concepts only; they have kept the notion of justice an idea or an ideal because this world has never experienced any lasting justice. On the one hand, we try to intellectualize justice, to show how laws of just societies protect what is interpreted as being 'just' and how a politically organized society supports this premise of what is justice. Yet such an interpretation assumes that all societies are equal, that not only the demands of the individual must be met but the demands of the State cannot be ignored. But doesn't this sound familiar ? As Bahá'ís we know we are all equal, but not all the same. We all have needs but we don't have the same needs. We know that all States should be equal but they are at different stages of development. So how can we define justice by something that we have not yet developed? We are acknowledging that true justice does not yet exist in this world, but that it is something which we are working towards.

In working on a Bahá'í model for the future, it has been stated that we need to create laws and institutions that are universal in character. The future role of lawyers is to ensure that law is used as an effective tool in achieving this task. Law is the servant of justice, which means that lawyers are true servants of humanity. Areas of concern for lawyers include human rights. The rights of the individual must be protected, but not at the cost of the rights of the State. Future lawyers need to work towards an understanding of how the rights of the individual and the State coalesce within the Bahá'í framework. What institutions will be created to ensure these rights are protected? What happens if these laws are challenged or broken? These are the questions that lawyers in the future need to address. And what will be the outcome? Unity. Bahá'u'lláh said that 'the purpose of justice is the appearance of unity among men'.[6]

In order to obtain justice, there must be consultation. For lawyers this is no easy task. Lawyers are used to working in an adversarial or litigious environment. Being able to present a viewpoint or an argument that is more sound, more convincing than one's opponent is often proof of one's success as a lawyer. Being more eloquent, more articulate than another has been the hallmark of a true professional. But no more will eloquence or the power to persuade be the criteria by which lawyers in the future will be judged. All members of society must somehow be able to express their needs, but not their wishes; this is how the true art of consultation will be implemented by the lawyers. Bahá'u'lláh stated that we should 'bestow upon them according to their needs . . . deal with them with undeviating justice, so that none among them may either suffer want, or be pampered with luxuries. This is but manifest justice.'[7]

Next, the equality of the sexes will be an issue, as well as the relationships between individuals at all levels, including within families, and towards society as a whole, bearing in mind that what will be done will be for the highest good of the Bahá'í Faith. What is needed are acts of individuals which will be good for the community. And if it is good for the community, it will be good for the individual.

Another area that has yet to reach its true potential is the area relating to how nations interact. Here we are looking at the issue of international justice. At no other time in history have we been so able to look at the effects of one nation upon another. In Bosnia, 130,000 people were killed in 1992. In 1994, after UN intervention, less than 3,000 people were killed. Admittedly there are a number of ways of viewing these statistics, but it is very difficult to determine the impact of acts or omissions without looking at these statistics.

One reason that each nation is so much more involved in the affairs of other nations is that countries can react so much more quickly than they could in the past. Technology has changed our lives in ways that were perhaps unimaginable only twenty years ago. CNN lets us watch history as it happens. For the first time countless numbers of people were able to watch the 1991 Gulf War as it happened. The full horrors of war could be witnessed on a daily level. We could also witness the fall of Communism, the dissolution of the Soviet Union, the failed coup in Moscow. We didn't have to wait to read about it, we saw it as it happened—though perhaps we saw a biased view of some events as well. We now have a world in which we can communicate with each other so easily and we also have another means for misinformation to be spread. Certainly there are resource implications which mean that not all of us have the technology that is available, but it does exist.

Shoghi Effendi, in *The World Order of Bahá'u'lláh*, stated that: 'A mechanism of world inter-communication will be devised, embracing the whole planet, freed from national hindrances and restrictions, and functioning with marvellous swiftness and perfect regularity.'[8] We already have the dirt road that takes us to this level of communication: the internet. We need to learn more about how it functions to ensure that the rights of the State are protected so that it cannot be abused to create the Orwellian nightmare foretold in *Nineteen Eighty Four*. And we also need lawyers who are experts in the field of communications, journalism and copyright laws, who can draft laws for the new world, laws that ensure true justice for the individual and the State.

Bahá'u'lláh's world commonwealth, consisting of a legislature, an executive and a judiciary system, will create much scope for lawyers attuned to ensuring justice for the world. Both the League of Nations and the Charter of the United Nations should be seen as building blocks upon which the new commonwealth will be founded. But we need to learn from the mistakes of this century—and there have been many: the power of veto given to members of the security council; the peace-keeping as opposed to peace-making powers of the UN; the lack of an international police force; the lack of power to punish those who do not pay their dues; the non-interference mandate ensuring that lawless States can ride rough-shot over their constituents; these are but a few of the flaws inherent in the Charter of the United Nations.

Lawyers need to be visionaries, to have a realistic feel for the future world order. If we are to participate in the advancement of the peoples of this planet, to be part of the solution we need to study some aspect of the changes that are necessary. Armed with such knowledge, we can be true participants and help ensure that our planet passes through this painful episode in its life, and onto a brighter future.

Other areas that need attention include taxation, one of the two certainties of life that will still be with us in the next century. International taxation will become a new issue, and we will still have domestic taxation in all its varied and beautiful forms! No-one willingly agrees to additional taxation, so the new model of the world requires a drastic change in people's behaviour. Who knows what the world must endure before an international tax will be accepted universally? If we study all the issues that require a funda-mental shift in individual behaviour, there can only be one conclusion reached about how such a change in behaviour can arise, with a concomitant change in attitudes. It is to this point that I direct my comment about the need for an upheaval of unprecedented proportions that must occur in order for the necessary changes to take place. Much has been written about the dire warnings to the peoples of the earth about what is in our short term future unless we make a change spontaneously and without any external pressures. If wars, natural disasters, terrorism and racism at the levels witnessed in recent years in Bosnia and Rwanda, let alone the daily more subtle, but equally obnoxious, attacks on people of different races in countries such as the United States, Australia and Germany, to name but a few, have not been sufficient to change the hearts of the peoples of this planet, what ordeals does humanity have to endure to ensure this change occurs?

There is much to do for lawyers, these new servants of humanity. And much can be done now. We know what will happen in the future: not the details, but the framework. We don't know how it will come about but we do know it will come soon. Time is running out and we can be at the vanguard of this new age that awaits us. The promise of the new world offers much for lawyers and may well witness the true coming of age of the legal profession as a truly honourable profession in the world, one of which we will be proud to be a part.

Notes & references

The views expressed in this paper are those of the author, and are not to be interpreted as representing the view of the Bahá'í World Centre.
1. Bahá'u'lláh, *Gleanings from the Writings of Bahá'u'lláh*, comp. and trans. Shoghi Effendi, rev. ed. (London: Bahá'í Publishing Trust, 1978), CXVII, p. 249.
2. Alan Dershowitz, 'The Politically Correct Law School', *ABA Journal*, Sep. 1991, p. 53.
3. Bahá'í International Community Office of Public Information, *The Prosperity of Humankind* (London: Bahá'í Publishing Trust, 1995), p. 6.
4. Ibid., p. 8.
5. Ibid., p. 9.

6. Bahá'u'lláh, *Tablets of Bahá'u'lláh revealed after the Kitáb-i-Aqdas*, comp. Research Department of the Universal House of Justice, trans. Habib Taherzadeh with the assistance of a Committee at the Bahá'í World Centre, 1st US hardcover ed. (Wilmette, Ill: Bahá'í Publishing Trust, 1993), p. 67.

7. Bahá'u'lláh, *Gleanings*, CXIV, p. 234.

8. Shoghi Effendi, *The World Order of Bahá'u'lláh: Selected Letters,* 1st pocket-sized ed. (Wilmette, Ill: Bahá'í Publishing Trust, 1991), p. 203.

THE UNIVERSALITY OF HUMAN RIGHTS, TOLERANCE AND FREEDOM OF RELIGION

Pieter van Dijk

THE UNITED NATIONS proclaimed 1995 'The Year of Tolerance', therefore it seemed appropriate to make the concept of tolerance the central theme of this presentation. It seemed even more appropriate because of the central place that tolerance has in the Bahá'í Faith.

Before I go into a number of legal aspects of tolerance in relation to human rights in general and the freedom of religion in particular, I wish to stress that the non-legal aspects of the issue are also important: perhaps even more so. Especially for a lawyer, this is sometimes difficult to accept, but, nonetheless, important to recognize. In actual fact, there are many non-legal methods which may be highly instrumental in promoting and protecting human rights. As Clark notes with respect to intolerance: 'It is easier to legislate to change the discriminatory patterns of behaviour than it is to change attitudes of mind—as the history of civil rights laws in many countries indicates. This is not to suggest that the law has no deterrent or educative effects. It is only to suggest that changing the bad laws or introducing laws prohibiting certain activities is only a partial solution of the problem. Other educational techniques must be tried as well.'[1] Teaching and exchange of information in the field of human rights should be directed towards the awareness both of one's own rights and entitlement to equal treatment and tolerance, and of the rights and entitlements of others.

Beginning with young children, education should be a continuing process in which the issues to be discussed and the messages to be conveyed must be adapted to the age and level of education of the target group. It also includes training people in becoming aware of human rights issues in their daily lives—both private and professional—and of the possibilities that exist for everyone in his or her personal situation for helping solve problems and taking affirmative action. Both education (in the more academic sense) and training require the availability of, and free access to, information which is adequate for the goals to be served, and adapted to the age and level of education of the person concerned.

This need for education and information not only applies to potential victims of intolerance, but equally to judges, lawyers, law-enforcing authorities, prison staff etc. Their functioning, attitudes and action can prevent the necessity of international procedures, and are indispensable for the implementation of the outcome of these procedures at the domestic level. In the UN convention against torture, education, instruction and information as preventive measures are even incorporated as a State obligation in Article 10. And

1993 World Conference on Human Rights even devotes a separate section to human rights education. In Article 78 of Part II it is stated: 'The World Conference on Human Rights considers human rights education, training and public information essential for the promotion and achievement of stable and harmonious relations among communities and for fostering mutual understanding, tolerance and peace.'

For the enforcement, and especially for a uniform interpretation and application of the international human rights standards, it is important that members of the national judiciary regularly attend international meetings and seminars where issues of interpretation and application are discussed, and where they can exchange experiences and may find solutions for problems with which they have been confronted.

At the same time, the role of the non-governmental organizations ('NGOs') should be stressed. Their close connection with the beneficiaries of effective implementation of human rights standards make them appropriate initiators and performers of programmes directed at creating awareness of, and mobilizing action for, these human rights.

Special attention should be given to the role of the media in educating society in the spirit of tolerance. Indeed they have the power—intentionally or unintentionally—to manipulate reality, but they can at the same time contribute to the suppression of prejudice and expansion of intolerance.[2] It is, therefore, important that the media are briefed and provided with information to give their collaborators an appropriate understanding of situations and causes which might help them avoid using stereotypes and pejorative or discriminative terminology, thereby stirring up intolerance. They should, on the contrary, convince their audience that tolerance is not only desirable from a moral point of view, but has a positive effect on the life of the individual and the society.

Compatibility of universality and tolerance

Tolerance constitutes such an essential element of respect for human rights, that a claim for such respect unaccompanied by an attitude of tolerance seems insincere, or at least unjustified.

Additionally, it should be stated that an appeal to tolerance loses credibility when it originates from a person or institution as a defence against the reproach that this very person or institution itself shows a lack of tolerance. A person suspected of theft who would, before court, appeal to tolerance with respect to his own pattern of values regarding property rights would, of course, be confronted with the counter argument that he is trying to avoid a norm to which he should submit as a member of society, and that his appeal to tolerance is prompted by personal opportunism, and does not take into account his fellow citizens and their possessions; in its essence tolerance concerns a mutual give-and-take.

The authorities of States accused of human rights violations, when confronted with this argument, could argue that their regimes are tolerant to other States and do not hinder them from complying with their own pattern of values. In doing so they would be overlooking the fact that exactly when international norms with respect to human rights are involved, this does not only involve tolerance *among* States, but also the observance of tolerance *within* the State. And there, the perspective of the victim and that of the ruler may be worlds apart.[3] Therefore, two different sides to the concept of tolerance are confounded in this 'dialogue of the deaf'. In the area of international protection of human rights, tolerance with respect to the individual and his basic values should be placed to the fore. As it was observed by Van Boven: 'What transpires is that the victim's perspective is a more telling and more convincing testimony of common values and common aspirations shared by humankind than the pretentious arguments of religious and secular leaders (often oppressors) who deny or confound the universal character of the concept of human rights.'[4]

But when the situation within the State is involved, is there not a stronger case for an appeal to that State's own pattern of values? Is it not possible that individuals who, from a Western pattern of values, are regarded as victims of human rights violations, and as oppressed, are criminal offenders, or involved in undermining State security according to the pattern of values of the State concerned?

Even if such an auto-interpretation is acceptable from an anthropological point of view, and morally acceptable as to its ultimate implications,[5] then still the answer provided by international law on this issue is that also the scope which a national political system leaves for interpreting and limiting internationally recognized rights and freedoms with respect to the individuals residing under their own jurisdiction, is something which directly concerns other States. One of the results brought about by developments which occurred in the community of States during the last decades is precisely that the relationship between government and citizens is no longer exclusively a domestic issue belonging to the *domaine reservée* of the State, but has also become an issue of 'international concern'. Not only States, but also the citizens of these States, are entitled to tolerance, if not according to national law, then at least to international law. As far as tolerance can be regarded as equal to non-intervention, it is limited by these international developments, which in the area of human rights have largely deprived the claim for non-intervention of its foundations.[6] The Vienna Declaration and Programme of Action, which was adopted on 25 June 1993 by consensus at the Second World Conference on Human Rights, also states in so many words that 'the promotion and protection of all human rights is a legitimate concern of the international community.'

The pattern of values used for judging who is the oppressor and who the oppressed, will then not exclusively be determined by national culture and national law, but ultimately by international law, in so far as that contains binding norms for the States concerned. And also the way in which the State 'translates' these international norms into the national situations, is not exclusively the domain of the sovereign will of that State, because this would affect the effectiveness of these standards. Indeed, in 'translating' these norms, States would be easily inclined to manipulate these norms according to the wishes and interests of the authorities. Especially in the case of norms in the area of human rights, human needs and interests should take precedence over the *raison d'état* as a guideline in the determination of their content and scope.[7] The United Nations initiative to draft an international Bill of Human Rights embodying universal norms was also particularly a reaction against excesses of State sovereignty and universal values.

Apart from that, if one views each of the internationally recognized human rights separately, one may wonder if opinions about validity and content of the rights really differ so much. Certainly in the case of the core rights, which will be dealt with later on, and which go to the nub of human existence and human dignity, this is not quite so obvious, particularly given the fact that the core is hardly if at all determined by culture, especially from the perspective of the subject of those rights. One does not have to be a Kantian to call into question whether opinions about righteousness and human dignity differ so much among the States that these differences go to the heart of internationally recognised human rights.[8] In that context it is also significant that non-western, regional documents with respect to human rights do not fundamentally differ from the Universal Declaration of Human Rights.[9]

Whatever the case may be as to the existence and range of relativity of values and its impact on the problem of universality, in international law concerning human rights that impact has decreased as a consequence of developments described above with respect to the international adoption and supervision of human rights norms after World War II, which led to normative and functional universality. On the basis of consensus among the members of the community of States, those differences of values are considered either to have lost their relevance for these norms or to have been integrated in these norms.

Compatibility of the universal character of norms with differences in their interpretation and implications

Universality of human rights does not exclude the possibility of a certain differentiation in interpretation of these rights. This is not the case, first of all, due to the fact that universality does not imply that formulated norms are completely unequivocal on all counts. Secondly, universally valid norms do not require uniformity in all respects in their application. Nevertheless, it is very important to emphasise the following two points regarding this issue:

If, and as far as, a norm has received international recognition, variations must not affect the essence of that norm; there is only little scope for the interpretation of the norm and—maybe a little more—for variations with regard to the national implementation.

Within the context of normative and functional universality, it is up to the international community as a last resort, within the framework of international norms and through international supervision, to define the scope for these variations.

One right leaves more scope for variations in the interpretation and implementation than another, because for certain rights a differentiated implementation affects the universal validity of the norm in its essence, while this does not have to be so for other rights. In this respect I think it would be useful to classify the human rights in certain categories, namely: 1) core rights; 2) participation rights; and 3) other rights.[10]

'Core rights' encompass those rights without which human existence would be impossible, both mentally and physically: right to life and an adequate standard of living (Articles 3 and 25); the right to personal liberty and security of person (Article 3); prohibition of slavery and servitude (Article 4); prohibition of torture and cruel inhuman or degrading treatment and punishment (Article 5); prohibition of arbitrary detention (Article 9); prohibition of discrimination (Articles 1 and 2); the right to recognition as a person before the law (Article 6); prohibition of the retrospective force of penalties (Article 11); freedom of thought, conscience and religion (Article 18). That these rights concern

195

the very core of human rights is indicated by the fact that almost all of them have been listed in paragraph 2 of Article 4 of the International Covenant on Civil and Political Rights, meaning that they are embodied as rights of which no derogation is possible even in case of a public emergency.

'Participation rights' are those rights the exercise of which must be guaranteed at least at a minimum level to ensure full enjoyment of the core rights, and to enable the person concerned to claim this full enjoyment personally. Next to this supporting function, these rights also have a value of their own with respect to human dignity. One could think of the following rights: the right to take part in the government of the country and the right to periodic and secret elections (Article 21); the right to participate in the country and to maintain and develop his own cultural identity;[11] and the right to education (Articles 26 and 27); the freedom to manifest one's religion or belief and the right to free expression (Articles 18 and 19); the right to assembly and association, including the freedom to join trade unions (Articles 20 and 25); and the right to effective legal aid in the case of violations of fundamental rights, access to a court, the right to a fair trial in the determination of rights and obligations and respect of the presumption of innocence (Articles 8, 10 and 11). As far as the exercise of these rights is not indispensable for the full enjoyment of one or more core rights, no absolute value can be attached to them. If the law provides so, this exercise may be submitted to certain limitations in order to protect the rights of others or to protect certain public interests.

It is possible to hold different views on the precise classification into categories as suggested here.[12] I wish merely to emphasise that one should not put all these norms on the same line when dealing with the question of whether, and to what extent, universal norms concerning human rights leave scope for different interpretations and applications by various States on the grounds of political, economical, cultural, or other differences. In the case of the core rights, there is little scope for variation, in so far as in the norm concerned there are terms open to different interpretations in different circumstances. Thus the right to life implies a prohibition of an arbitrary deprivation of life, while the question whether arbitrariness occurs in a certain case may depend on the circumstances, place and time. And even the concept of 'life' is in certain cases susceptible to different interpretations which have not been excluded as yet by an 'autonomous' international interpretation, as national and international case law regarding abortion and euthanasia have shown.[13] The same applies to the question whether in a specific case a certain treatment constitutes torture and whether or not this is inhuman or degrading. Different interpretations of values and their mutual order can exert a certain influence, without detracting from the norm itself.

In the case of participation rights, there is more scope for influencing their interpretation and application in view of differences in opinions on values and orders within the framework of the weighting of the interests on which the application of the explicit or inherent limitations has to be based. The 'margin of discretion' usually left to the States by the international supervisory bodies and courts,[14] may be regarded as a universally valid characteristic of these norms. Additionally, there is also scope here for a multi-cultural interpretation of certain concepts, for instance the concept of 'family' in Article 16.[15]

How universal is freedom of religion?

The right to freedom of thought, conscience and religion is guaranteed under international law without qualifications; no derogations or limitations are allowed. It may be true that thoughts and convictions become valuable for the person concerned only if he is allowed to express them; this does not render the freedom of thought as such without meaning. The international guaranteed freedom also implies that one cannot be subjected to a treatment intended to change the process of thinking, or be forced to express one's thoughts, to divulge or change one's religious opinion. Moreover, it implies that no sanction may be put on holding a certain political opinion or religious belief, which also may not constitute a ground for unfavourable treatment. This makes the freedom of thought and religion an absolute freedom which, in its absolute form, is universal in character and leaves no room for a different interpretation on the grounds of a different value system, a different economic system, a different political situation, or whatever differences there may be. On the contrary, freedom of thought and religion is intended precisely also to protect those who do not share the ruling political or religious convictions and, in essence, requires tolerance and respect for each others' views.

Freedom of expression and the right to manifest one's religion, on the other hand, have direct implications for the rights of others. One only has to think of the right to have one's reputation protected against defamation, the right to be protected against scandalous magazines, the right not to be confronted against one's will by pornographic publications, and the right not to be hurt in one's deepest religious feelings. Moreover, the freedom of expression and the right to manifest one's religion may come in conflict with certain general interests which the State is supposed to protect, like State secrecy and national security, public morals, prevention of crime and disorder, and the maintenance of the impartiality of the judiciary. This means that the freedom of expression and the right to manifest one's religion cannot be of an absolute character, because that would automatically place the other rights and public interests mentioned on a second level. That is why the human rights treaties provide that the exercise of freedom of expression and the right to manifest one's religion may be restricted by law to the extent necessary in a democratic society for the protection of those other rights and interests. It is clear that the necessity requirement opens the way for differences of opinion about which restrictions are, under the given circumstances in a country or in a region or in a city or village, necessary to protect the rights of others or the general interest.

The European Court of Human Rights has adopted the view that, in principle , the national or local authorities are in a better position to assess the situation and to determine the necessity of certain restrictions than an international court. For that reason, it leaves those authorities what is called a 'margin of discretion' in that respect. On the other hand, the European Court has emphasized that the way in which the authorities exercise that discretion will be supervised by the Court, since otherwise the international guarantee of the freedom of expression would become meaningless. When exercising its international supervision, however, the Court, for its part, will take into consideration differences between countries. First of all, as the court held in the Handyside case,[16] concepts of morals are not necessarily common in all countries. Moreover, the requirements of national security may differ depending on the actual political situation of the country. Wether a certain expression, for instance a protest or political campaign may predictably create disorder, also depends on the situation of that particular moment.

Conclusion

The recognition of existing differences between peoples and societies, and of the indispensable value of tolerance with respect to these differences, does not result in denial of the universal validity of norms under the current state of international law. But it does provide a foundation for the claim that these norms must not necessarily be interpreted and implemented universally with regard to all their elements; neither considered on their own, nor in a mutual balancing of norms. On the other hand, Article 30 of the Universal Declaration of Human Rights indicates that no right may be interpreted in such a way as would lead to the destruction of any other rights and freedoms; in such a case the situation is a matter of balance: for example, balancing the right to freedom of speech with the right to respect for freedom of religion (which necessarily includes respect for the religious convictions of others). In the absence of consensus, the scales may be set by different patterns of values. In fundamentally religious communities, respect for religious conviction will limit the exercise of freedom of opinion, while in a secular society, more value will be attached to freedom of speech, unless the goal of expression clearly and exclusively is to offend the religious convictions of others. These differences seem justifiable and only subject to marginal international review. But when this balancing leads to a measure that affects a person's core right to life, as in the affair of Salman Rushdie, Article 30 applies and international intervention would be justifiable.

It also implies that in the case of international supervision the laws will be enforced on other States from a unilateral (e.g. West European) pattern of values. When the Chinese spokesman said at the Second World Conference in Vienna: 'Thus, one should not and cannot think of the human rights standard as a model of certain countries as the only proper ones and demand all other countries to comply with them', he was certainly right. The international supervision should not take the value patterns of certain States, but universal patterns of value as its starting point.

We must search for the solution to the tension between universality and the relativity of values by an independent and impartial international supervision of the implementation of the universal norms by the States. With this postulate of independence and impartiality, the jurist finds himself on familiar ground, because this is closely related to the principle of due process and fair trail.

Notes & references

This paper is partly based upon an article published in the *Netherlands Quarterly of Human Rights*, 1995, no. 3.

1. R.S. Clark, Models of National or Local Action to Prevent or Combat Intolerance of Religion or Belief, UN Doc HR/GENEVA/1984/BP.3, p. 6.

2. See R.S. Verebalavu, 'The Role of the Media', in *Congress Resolutions, Conscience and Liberty*, 1993.

3. See Th. C. van Boven 'General Course on Human Rights', *Collected Courses of the Academy of European law 1993*, vol. IV-2, 1995, pp. 1-106 (p. 22).

4. Ibid., pp. 12-13.

5. It is difficult to indicate exactly where the limit is, except for extreme cases. See, on this subject, C. Kluckhohn, 'Ethical relativity: Sic et non', *Journal of Philosophy*, 1995, pp. 663-77.

6. See A. Bloed and P. van Dijk, 'Human Rights and Non-Intervention', in A. Bloed and P. van Dijk (eds), *Essays on Human Rights in the Helsinki Process* (Dordrecht: Martinus Nijhoff Publishers, 1985), pp. 57-78.

7. See P. van Dijk and G van Hoof, *Theory and Practice of the European Convention on Human Rights*, 2nd edition (Deventer: Kluwer, 1990), p. 605. Compare also S. Prakash Sinah, 'The Anthropo-centric Theory of International Law as a Basis for Human Rights', *Case Western Reserve Journal of International Law*, 1978, pp. 469-502.

8. J. Donnelly, 'Cultural Relativism and Universal Human Rights', *Human Rights Quarterly* 1984, pp. 400-19 (p. 400). See also P. Baehr, *The Role of Human Rights in Foreign Policy* (Basingstoke: Houndmills, 1994), pp. 15-16; and T. Wilson, 'A Bedrock Consensus for Human Rights', in A. Henkin (ed), *Human Dignity: The Internationalization of Human Rights* (New York: Aspen Institute of Human Rights, 1979), pp. 47-63 (p. 63).

9. A. Cassese, *Human Rights in a Changing World* (Cambridge: Polity Press, 1990), pp. 66-7, referring to the African Charter of 1981 and the Islamic Declarations of 1981 and 1986.

10. P. van Dijk, 'Rechten van de Mens en Onwikkelingssamenwerking: enige rechtsbeginselen' ['Human Rights and Development Cooperation; Some Legal Principles'], *NJCM-Bulletin*,1980, pp. 4-20 (pp.12-14).

11. This is an addition which has not explicitly been included in Article 27 of the Universal Declaration, but may be inferred through an interpretation on the basis of Article 27 of the International Covenant on Civil and Political Rights.

12. See G. van Hoof, 'Human rights in a Multi-Cultural World: The need for continued Dialogue' in R. MacDonald (ed.), *Essays in Honour*

of Wang Tieya (Dordrecht: Martinus Nijhoff Publishers, 1994), pp. 877-91, who compares some classifications, and, by way of conclusion, presents a list of core rights.

13. See P. Smits, *The Right to Life of the Unborn Child in International Documents, Decisions and Opinions* (academic dissertation, Leiden University, 1992).

14. See, for the Strasbourg case law referring to the European Convention on Human Rights, Van Dijk and Van Hoof, op. cit., pp. 538-606.

15. Strasbourg case law has emphasised the autonomous meaning of this concept for Article 8 of the European Convention, which indicates a meaning which is independent of the prevailing views of the separate States, but on the other hand it has created scope for cultural differences. This way, for instance, polygamy and the marriage ceremony conducted in accordance with a certain cultural tradition have been recognized as the basis for founding a 'family'. European Commission of Human Rights, admissability decision on Appl. 299/66, Kahn v. United Kingdom, Yearbook X (1967), p. 478; European Court of Human Rights, judgement of 28 May 1985, Abdulaziz, Cabales en Balkandali, ECHR Series A.94 (1985), p. 32.

16. European Court of Human Rights, judgment of 7 December 1976, Handyside, ECHR Series A.24 (19786), p. 22.

ABOUT THE AUTHORS

Kiser Barnes was born in Baltimore, Maryland, USA. He became a Bahá'í in 1974, and in 1976 pioneered to the Republic of Benin where he was elected to the National Spiritual Assembly. In 1980 he pioneered to Ife, Nigeria, and served there as a member of the Auxiliary Board for nine years. In 1990 he was appointed to the Continental Board of Counsellors for Africa, and later to the International Teaching Centre, moving to the Bahá'í World Centre in 1993. His qualifications include a BA degree from Morgan State University; Juris Doctor, University of Maryland; and an MPhil in Law, Obafemi Awolowo University. As a lawyer he has specialized in constitutional and human rights issues affecting African-Americans and women, and, as a professor of law, has held senior posts in both the USA and Africa. He has also worked as a journalist, a consultant on race relations, and a television commentator.

Colleen Dawes has worked for the Australian Parliament House's Research Service as a specialist in international and taxation law and for the Australian Department of Foreign

Affairs' International Law Division in the area of treaty negotiation, with particular reference to nuclear arms, international trade and international taxation treaties. She later taught Taxation and Commercial Law at Flinders University, and has worked as a tax consultant for a major Australian law firm. Since becoming a Bahá'í she has served on local, regional and national Bahá'í committees and also as the Legal Officer for the National Spiritual Assembly of the Bahá'ís of Australia. In 1990 she moved to the Bahá'í World Centre in Israel, to head the Office of Legal Affairs, which advises the Universal House of Justice. She has presented a number of papers on legal ethics and justice to Bahá'í conferences and has written several articles published in Australian law journals.

Peter van Dijk is a member of the Council of State of the Netherlands. He is a distinguished public servant, and among his many civic duties he serves as Deputy Justice of the Court of Justice at The Hague; Member of the Board of Appeal for Trade and Industry; Member of the Advisory Committee for International Legal Questions; Chairman of the Netherlands Institute of Human Rights; Chairman of the Board of The Foundation on Inter-Ethnic Relations; General Secretary of the Netherlands Helsinki Committee. After completing his law studies at the University of Utrecht in 1966, Dr van Dijk received a doctorate in law (*cum laude*) from the University of Leiden. From 1967-76 he taught at the Faculty of Law, University of Utrecht, and, from 1976-90, was Professor of International Organizations at the Europa Institute. His academic achievements include Fulbright scholarships and visiting professorships to a number of prestigious universities including Columbia, Michigan and Harvard in the USA.

Wendi Momen holds a BSc in Economics and a PhD in International Relations, both from the London School of Economics. Her thesis was 'The Foreign Policy and Relations of The Gambia' (1977). She has worked as a freelance editor since 1979, primarily for George Ronald, Publisher. She has served as a magistrate (Justice of the Peace) in the criminal court since 1982, and as a court chairman since 1994. She was appointed to the family panel (domestic) in 1984, and has been a court chairman of this panel since 1991. In 1990 she was appointed a non-executive director of Bedfordshire Family Health Services Authority and of Bedfordshire Health Authority in 1994. She has served on the National Spiritual Assembly of the Bahá'ís of the United Kingdom since 1982, as treasurer from 1984 to 1990, and as chairman since 1990. Dr Momen has been married to Moojan Momen since 1971. They have two adult children.

Udo Schaefer, born in 1926, joined the Bahá'í Faith a few years after the Second World War. After studies in musicology and Latin, he studied law at Heidelberg University, where he took his degrees. The subject of his doctoral thesis was the Constitutional Law of the Bahá'í Community in comparison with Canon Law and Protestant Church Law. He worked as a chief public-prosecutor at the State Court of Heidelberg, retiring form this post in 1988. He is author of several works on the Bahá'í Faith, which have been published in German, English, French, Spanish, Russian, Dutch and Persian translations. He is a member of the National Spiritual Assembly of the Bahá'ís of Germany.

Christopher Sprung studied law at the University of Mainz, Germany. His interests are in constitutional and international laws, human rights and the United Nations. He is active as an attorney assisting in the recognition of Bahá'í communities, particularly in Eastern Europe, and in matters of citizenship and refugee status.Mr Sprung was born in 1955 and has been a Bahá'í since 1971, serving as a member of the National Spiritual Assembly of the Bahá'ís of Germany since 1979, and as its Secretary from 1985-95.

THE TÁHIRIH INSTITUTE

The Táhirih Institute is an educational foundation set up in 1989 by the National Spiritual Assembly of the Bahá'ís of the Netherlands to promote awareness and development of the qualities and virtues necessary to achieve world peace.

Bahá'ís work towards the creation of an ever-advancing sustainable world civilization based on the teachings of Bahá'u'lláh (1817-92), Founder of the Bahá'í Faith, who explained that there is only one religion, and that all of the Messengers of God have progressively revealed its nature. He also stated that, 'The well-being of mankind, its peace and security, are unattainable unless and until its unity is firmly established.' Recognizing the basic requirements of a lasting world peace, the Táhirih Institute seeks to promote the study and implementation of such principles as: world peace; the oneness of humankind; the unity of religion; the equality of men and women; universal education; the equality of races, classes and peoples; the harmony of science and religion; economic and social justice; and environmental protection.

The Institute's Board consists of experienced Bahá'ís from academic, scientific, cultural and managerial backgrounds. The Board often represents the Bahá'í community of the Netherlands in seminars, conferences and working parties with a variety of institutions and organizations

Táhirih was a poet and scholar in nineteenth century Persia, a fervent advocate of the equality of men and women, who became widely celebrated throughout Europe. She was persecuted for her beliefs, and executed in 1852 at the age of thirty-six. An important figure in the history of the Bahá'í Faith, her heroism and ideals continue to inspire millions of people around the world.